HILTON CARTER
LIVING WILD

HOW TO PLANT STYLE YOUR HOME & CULTIVATE HAPPINESS.

RYLAND PETERS & SMALL
LONDON · NEW YORK

This book is dedicated to Fiona and Holland.
I love you endlessly.

Photographer Hilton Carter
Senior designer Megan Smith
Senior editor Annabel Morgan
Art director Sally Powell
Creative director Leslie Harrington
Head of production Patricia Harrington

Published in 2023 by CICO Books
An imprint of Ryland Peters & Small Ltd
20–21 Jockey's Fields
London WC1R 4BW
and
341 E 116th Street
New York, NY 10029
www.rylandpeters.com

10 9 8 7 6 5 4 3 2 1

Text © Hilton Carter 2023
Design and photography
© CICO Books 2023

The author's moral rights have been asserted. All rights reserved. No part of this publication may be reproduced, stored in a retrieval system, or transmitted in any form or by any means, electronic, mechanical, photocopying, or otherwise, without the prior permission of the publisher.

A CIP catalog record for this book is available from the Library of Congress and the British Library.

ISBN: 978-1-80065-212-5

Printed in China

WINDOW DIRECTION AND LIGHT LEVELS
Understanding the type of light you have in your home will make a big difference to the choice of plants you can place in those areas. Here's a breakdown of the types of light your plants will receive in the northern hemisphere, depending on the direction in which a window is facing (these directions will be reversed if you live in the southern hemisphere):

NORTHERN EXPOSURE Medium to bright indirect light
NORTHEAST EXPOSURE Medium to bright indirect light. Depending on the time of year, direct sunlight in the morning
NORTHWEST EXPOSURE Bright indirect light
EASTERN EXPOSURE Direct morning sunlight to bright indirect light
SOUTHERN EXPOSURE Bright indirect light to medium light
SOUTHEAST EXPOSURE Bright indirect light
SOUTHWEST EXPOSURE Bright indirect light to direct afternoon sunlight
WESTERN EXPOSURE Bright indirect light to direct afternoon sunlight

CONTENTS

Introduction	6

DESIGNING A LIVING HOME 8

Light Works	12
Color Scheming	18
Mixing Materials	22
Perfect Planters	26
Living Walls	32
Centerpieces	38
Statement Plants	42
The Art of the Pedestal	48
Outdoor Glamour	52

DESIGNER PLANTS 62

STYLED SPACES: A PORTFOLIO OF FLORA 104

Poetic Planting	108
Artist's Statement	120
Wood Grains and Concrete Plains	130
A Room with a View	140
Mixed Greens	152
Neighbors	162
A Gathered Space	174
Untitled (The Painter and the Photographer)	186

STYLING A CHILD'S ROOM 198

Creating Joyful Spaces	200
Plants for Kids' Spaces	212
Index	222
Credits	224
Thanks and Love	224

LIVING WILD

HOW TO PLANT STYLE YOUR HOME & CULTIVATE HAPPINESS.

When WRITING this book, I saved the Introduction for last. Reason being, for one, that I had no idea how to introduce it, and two, because I was hoping that during the process of working my way through the 200 pages something would come to me. And clearly it worked, because here we are.

I knew from the moment that I finished writing my last book, *Wild Creations*, that if I was fortunate enough to have the opportunity to create another, it would be about plant styling and design. Over the years I've provided tools to help those in the plant-loving community keep their plants happy and thriving while dabbling in a bit of styling here and there. In my first book *Wild at Home*, I walked the novice plant lover through care and design tips, with a few fun projects woven in. Book number 2, *Wild Interiors*, took readers to different parts of the world to hear about the journeys in greenery of other plant lovers and provided tips on which plants work best in particular rooms. And in my third book, *Wild Creations*, I presented projects and hacks that would be fun to create at home and still found the time to get on my soapbox and rant about the importance of good plant parenting.

I spent my first three books preaching about providing plants with everything they need to thrive as well as the tangible benefits of living with plants. If you've read any of my previous books, you'll know just how passionate I am about understanding how to care for a plant before you have fun styling it. With all that essential information stored in your minds and hearts, in *Living Wild* it's finally time to get into the artistry of plant styling and learn how making the right design choices with plants can transform a space, and, at the end of the day, bring a sense of contentment and happiness.

Throughout this book, I share my ethos, if you will, and reveal the way I go about styling a space with plants. Starting with my own home and visiting residential and commercial spaces that I've plant styled along the way, I will take you on a deep dive into the reasoning behind my designs and decisions. You'll hear me talk about the power of color and texture, how to create a statement, and the art of the pedestal. I will challenge you to look at houseplants on an artistic level and reveal my favorite "designer plants" that help shape the way a room comes together, just as a rug or couch or piece of art might do. I want you to experience the appeal of clean modern lines being disrupted by wild organic forms and see how choosing one planter over another makes a world of difference.

These are just some of the themes you'll encounter within the pages of this book. My hope is that after reading it, you are able to apply these methods to your own space and move forward towards living wild. Enjoy.

DESIGNING A LIVING HOME

I'm often asked what my style is, and to be honest I never think about it when designing a room for myself or others. But if I was to stand back and look at it from a bird's-eye view, I guess I would describe it as "modern lush." Ok, that may not be a style you're familiar with, but I'm making it a thing. Modern Lush. It has a nice ring to it. My home is a mix of modern, Scandinavian, and Mexican influences all blended together, and once I add the plants, that's how modern lush is birthed. For me, the same energy and thoughtfulness that go into selecting the right color of paint for the walls, or the perfect pieces of furniture, should go into selecting the right plants, planters, and accessories necessary to make a room feel finished. Plant styling requires an eye for understanding exactly which particular colors and shapes will vibe with each other. In design you just can't plan accordingly, you must also plant accordingly. These things are necessary when designing a living home.

In my first book, *Wild at Home*, I discussed three plant-styling methods that replicate the way we interact with plants in nature: levels, layering, and grouping. In the wild, we see greenery at a variety of different levels—at our feet, at eye level, and above. Indoors, creating the same effect requires hanging plants and planters, placing plants on tables or pedestals, and styling plants on the floor. Layering plants harks back to the way they grow in nature. Different species grow on top and alongside one another, creating what we understand as a "jungle." Mixing and matching foliage of various shapes, sizes, and textures indoors creates a similar effect and gives a space a robust and lush feel. Lastly, grouping involves bringing like-minded plants together to create a theme or look. For example, if you were looking to make your living room feel like a cottage in the arid Arizona desert, you'd group drought-tolerant cacti together to replicate that look. To design a living home, you'll see me put these methods and many others to use. But it all starts and ends with light.

LIGHT WORKS

Whenever I take on a new plant-styling job, the first thing I pay attention to is the source and direction of light in the home. Light plays such an important role in the health and vibrancy of plant life that pretty much every plant-styling decision I make is based on it.

There are a few essential facts to establish. First of all, from which direction does natural daylight enter the interior? This is important, because the aspect of a room will dictate the quality of light that enters. A northern-facing room will never receive direct sunlight, so plants that require direct sun won't thrive there. Instead, I'd choose plants like ferns, peperomias, anthuriums, orchids, and alocasias.

The same principles apply when considering plants for a west-facing room. The sun is at its hottest in the afternoon, so once it finds its way through a west-facing window, it will be harmful to plants that don't like direct sun. In such a space, I'd go for cacti, succulents, ponytail palms, crotons, or olive trees. Another factor is whether there are any obstructions that block the light. South-facing windows provide the best (bright, indirect) light for plants, but if there is a large tree or building directly outside, it will dial down the quality of the light from bright to medium.

When my wife and I were looking for a new home, one of the most important things on my checklist was plenty of light from the right direction. When we initially took a walk through the house, I noted that the sunroom was south-facing. Not only was it south-facing, but there was nothing blocking that glorious light. At that moment, I knew this house would be our home.

During the renovation process, the light source in each room played a large role in the way I designed the space. When it came to the

SUNROOM BLOOM
When it came to styling our sunroom, I wanted to take everything that I find so amazing about conservatories and bring that look and feel to the space. The fact that this room gets such great light throughout the day makes it the perfect blend of outdoor and indoor.

interior design, my goal was to make use of every room. I wanted our home to feel alive in a way that would allow visitors to feel comfortable and enjoy every corner. While all the items in our home were purchased with purpose, nothing is so precious that we cannot enjoy it fully.

While the existing sunroom had south- and east-facing windows, they weren't large enough to allow the room to house the number of plants I wanted. Leading with a design style I call modern lush, my idea was to turn our sunroom into an indoor oasis and our own private sanctuary. So we removed the exterior walls and replaced them with large windows and doors. This allows direct morning sun to creep in from the east and bright indirect light to fill the room from the south throughout the day.

When you have a room full of light, you can style almost any plant there. I started by placing Frank, my fiddle-leaf fig, in the right corner of the room. Because of his size and shape, he is the statement plant here. If you've been on this

journey with me, you'll be well aware of my friend Frank and how he's anchored rooms in my life in the past. Below and around him, I placed a *Philodendron* 'Green Congo', a burgundy rubber tree (*Ficus elastica* 'Burgundy'), a *Monstera deliciosa*, and a *Philodendron giganteum* and *P. tuxtlanum* 'Tuxtla'. While these plants have flat color in common, the leathery shine of their leaves plays so well with the fluted leather accent chairs, and the different shapes and sizes of the foliage create a jungly effect. For a pop of color and pattern, I placed a variegated rubber tree at the base of the grouping and a *Philodendron* 'Birkin' on the terrazzo coffee table.

To the left side of the room, to add height and create a sense of being enveloped by foliage, I placed an Australian tree fern (*Dicksonia antarctica*) on a pedestal. Pedestals are a great way to elevate a plant, allowing it to grab attention, and here the tree fern forms a green

SUN KISSED

Seeing my wife, Fiona, and daughter, Holland, enjoying our sunroom is all I could ask for. Creating this oasis has helped cultivate happiness in my life (opposite above). Looking from the kitchen into the sunroom, you can see how the rooms mesh into each other (opposite below). In the kitchen, the countertop and shelves are kissed by direct sun throughout the day, highlighting the mix of materials we chose for this space. We moved the kitchen from the north to the south side of the house, following the light (right and below).

canopy over the accent chair below. I chose the molten-gold-effect planter to tie in with the other gold accents in this space. Beside this, I styled a living wall using ferns, bromeliads, orchids, and air plants. Mounted in or on cork, they create the effect of nature bursting through the walls and taking over an abandoned space.

My vision was for the sunroom, kitchen, powder room, and dining room to all work in sync with each other and you can see this in the color palette, slatted wood, concrete, and clay tile that these rooms share. When renovating, we moved the kitchen from the north to the south side of the house. My wife Fiona and I love to entertain, so we wanted an open-plan kitchen that is warm, bright, and inviting. As the sunroom is the statement room of our home, I let the kitchen breathe a little, styling it with smaller plants.

In the dining room, where formal dinners and gatherings are held, you see my inner minimalist at work. The natural light in here is dappled at best and low at worst, setting the perfect scene throughout the day. Once day turns to night, the dimmable light fixture above the table steps in. To keep this space free-flowing, I styled a bird of paradise plant (*Strelitzia reginae*) and *Philodendron* 'Rojo Congo' in the corners. The table can be easily accessed, but there's still a generosity and lushness to the room. For a centerpiece, I styled a small burgundy rubber tree (*Ficus elastica* 'Burgundy') in a concrete planter, dressing the top of the soil with stones for a clean finish.

In the living room, where Fiona will from time to time take a much-needed nap, an explosion of ideas, color, texture, and light all came together. And when it came to plant styling this room, the light and space dictated how I would go about it.

The windows here face north and east, so I worked in plants that tolerate medium to low light. There's not a lot of empty floor space, so I used the shelves, mantlepiece, and surfaces to style greenery. On the bookshelf I've arranged a ZZ plant (*Zamioculcas zamiifolia*), a rabbit's foot fern (*Davallia solida var. fejeensis*), a watermelon begonia (*Peperomia argyreia*), and a cascading moonlight pothos (*Scindapsus treubii* 'Moonlight'). Bringing vine plants into areas of the room where they can gracefully trail down is a great way to make a corner more interesting or to hide a spot that you're less excited about. I draped vine plants around the living room, from a satin pothos (*Scindapsus pictus* 'Argyraeus') and variegated *Hoya carnosa* on the mantle to a marble queen pothos (*Epipremnum aureum*) on the cabinet. On the floor, tucked into the corners, I chose snake plants (*Dracaena trifasciata*), ferns, ZZ plants, and a *Dieffenbachia* hybrid.

SOFT SETTINGS

The dining room gets its color from a painting by Jose Mertz and its life from the *Philodendron* 'Rojo Congo' in the corner (above). A mix of light, color, and texture in our living room (opposite). Comfort was key when designing each space and Fiona takes advantage by napping in the living room (left).

COLOR SCHEMING

When it came to designing our home, I started by observing the light for inspiration. From there, I pulled together my color palette as the foundation for everything that would be layered on top. Color plays such an important role in interior design. Whether you have a scheme for each room or the entire home, it can exude an emotion, an energy, and provoke a reaction that can be invaluable. In college, I took a course on color theory and was blown away by the idea that certain colors look completely different when they are placed next to each other. It wasn't just the colors changing that amazed me; it was also the understanding that the feeling a particular color inspired could also shift based on its proximity to another color. That "aha!" moment has never left me, and I've used that knowledge in every single project I've worked on since.

RICH SPIRIT
A corner in the guest room of our home is made cozy not only by the dimmed lighting, lounge chair, and pouffe, but also thanks to the color palette (opposite). I've used color blocking to add richness and depth to spaces where only a few small plants could be utilized (far left) and painted large works of art to serve the same purpose (left). Against a solid color, mixing in an array of plants will provide a tapestry of color and texture (below).

Understanding color theory can be extremely beneficial when styling a space. If you're looking to make a room feel peaceful, use calming hues such as pink, blue, gray, green, or white. On the other hand, using neon yellow or bright red can make a space feel more electric or energized.

I wanted our home to have a calm, soothing atmosphere, so that spending time there would feel like being swaddled and rocked in a house-size hammock. That's why I went with a palette of terra-cotta, gray, white, green, black, and cream. These muted tones run through and connect all the rooms in the house. You see them in the tiled flooring in the sunroom and the powder room, the cabinetry in the kitchen, and the planters throughout our home.

For the walls, I wanted a bright white that would make every room feel lighter and ensure the black-framed windows pop. However, I also made sure it was a warm white for that calming effect. When it came to mixing in green, I allowed the plants to provide that splash of color. With so many plants scattered throughout, there is a large presence of green that gives the home life.

ART WORKS
When a piece of furniture has a striking color and pattern, placing a complementary plant beside it doubles the effect (left). While you should have a color palette to guide styling decisions, using artwork to provide a wild splash of color and interest in a room goes a long way. In our kitchen, I've hung the work of Lolo Gem (in the foreground) and Alina Fassakhova (behind) to bring life to the gallery white walls (below left). In our sunroom, the mix of colors in the painting by Jose Mertz helps to make the bar area feel lush (opposite).

When styling houseplants, you'll mostly be working with the color green, but, luckily for us, they come in so many shades. The best way to get the most out of your plantscapes is to work in different shades of green. These variations add depth and contrast both between the plants and the other elements that surround them. So it's key to be selective when pushing plants next to each other, just as you would be when placing two paint colors side by side on a wall or two different patterns of throw pillows on a couch.

Being laissez-faire about plant styling can be as much of an energy sponge as painting your living room a cold, clinical, bright white. There must be a desire to design a living home. I wouldn't call my style "modern lush" if I didn't strive for my home to feel full, bright, and vibrant.

When using the styling method of layering, you're utilizing the color, shape, and pattern of foliage to create a certain look and feel within a room. Have you ever seen a *Cissus discolor* leaf against the foliage of a *Philodendron* 'Rojo Congo'? It's stunning. Let the colors in your plants influence the paints you cover your walls with, the furniture you place throughout your home, and even the art you put on display. Styling them in this way brings a richness and life into your space that will be felt immediately.

MIXING MATERIALS

After your color palette is finalized, getting the textures—or, should I say, the textural landscape—of your home well-manicured is necessary.

Weaving in a tapestry of mixed materials with different textures gives a home definition and depth. When we started on our home renovation, my vision was to make sure that my core thesis of bringing the outdoors in was represented in every way possible. And while having plants in the home will, of course, provide that look, it is color, texture, and light that pull it all together. So when considering the textural landscape of our home, I wanted it to feel as if it was drawn directly from nature.

When moving through our space, you'll experience a mix of concrete, red oak, glazed ceramics, wicker, clay, raw terra-cotta, and gold and black metal, from the glazed ceramic tile flooring to the clay planters and the gold cactus lamp to the amber glass tumblers. All of these elements play a key role in bringing the outdoors in. Their tones and textures are a constant reminder of nature and create the warm feel that we typically describe as home.

When plant styling, playing around with plants that have contrasting textures and patterns will support the other natural materials in your home. Just as the colors in your plants should vary, the same goes for their textures. Styling a rubber tree (*Ficus elastica*) next to a *Philodendron rugosum* will bring the best out of both plants. While the leaves of the rubber tree have an almost patent-leather sheen, the *rugosum* is rugged and leathery. Experimenting with different textures in this way will create a sense of depth in any area of your home. There's a push and pull that will occur, a dynamic contrast that makes the space vibrate. The key is to stay curious and creative, so that when you're sitting in your home, enjoying the life that you've breathed into it, you feel that the time you spent searching for exactly the right textures was well worth it.

MIXED BAG
The gold cactus lamp in our sunroom shines bright—literally (above). In our kitchen, a mix of wood grain, clay, concrete, and glass is layered on the countertop and floating shelves (left). The sunroom is also a mixed bag of colors, textures, patterns, and materials. Each piece was painstakingly picked to bring out the beauty in the piece next to it (opposite).

WARM GLOW

Throughout our home, we have dimmable lighting that can instantly change the mood to warm and intimate. For me, it's important that our fixtures look unique and sculptural, blending perfectly into the design (above left). Portable lamps are the perfect addition to shelves or a tabletop to add a warm glow (left). A peek into our dining room shows the mix of natural materials that reflects the outdoor world. The light fixture was custom-made from walnut wood to match the chairs, while the concrete table was custom-made to match the kitchen island and countertop (above).

PERFECT ACCENTS

Wood is one of the strongest textures you can use in interior design as its warm tones and texture constantly bring us back to nature. When designing our home, I wanted to see wood grain running through from one room to another, as it does in the wild. Here is a detail of the red oak slats on the ceiling of the sunroom (left). I wanted a subtle gold accent to add a clean transition from the wood floors of the kitchen to the tile floor in the powder room (below left). The powder room continues many of the themes and materials seen throughout the house: slatted walls, a concrete vanity, a gold faucet/tap, clay tile flooring, and terra-cotta planters (below).

PERFECT PLANTERS

There are so many remarkable plants to bring into your home. So many variations in color and size, foliage and flowers, and growth patterns. It's the unique way each plant grows, based on the light and care that it receives, that makes every one special. But sometimes a plant can't do all the heavy lifting on its own. It needs a little extra sauce to show off its flavor. What I'm hinting at is finding the perfect planter. The pot. The vessel. The base. Whatever you call it, it will hold everything together and show off your personal aesthetic at the same time. Quite frankly, there is no true styling of a plant without providing it with the perfect planter. The planter is to the plant as the shirt is to the pants or as the dress is to the shoes. Both are great on their own, yes, but when the two come together, styled as one single outfit, they produce perfection.

Just as it's important only to bring in plants that can thrive in the light conditions your space provides, it is also crucial to give that plant a pot made from the right material. For example, if you own a cactus or *Ficus* that needs its soil to dry out quickly after each watering, you'll want to place it in a porous container made of concrete, clay, or terra-cotta. But if it's a plant such as a *Peperomia* that is looking to have its soil stay a little on the moist side, it will be happiest in a plastic, metal, or glazed ceramic container that will help retain moisture. This is one of the basics of plant care and once you have that established, then you can have fun with styling. Believe me, there is no fun in styling a beautiful new plant in an incredible planter just to have the plant die because you didn't place it in the proper light or your planter was made from the wrong material.

DRESS CODES
The planter is the outfit in which you dress your plant. Some perfect pairings include a *Philodendron* 'Jungle Boogie' dressed in a chunky ribbed planter (above right), a *Calathea setosa* in a *nerikomi*-style pot by Fay Ray Clay (right), and a *Philodendron* 'Birkin' in a Hilton Carter for Target planter (opposite).

FLOOR FIXTURES
Zoey sits next to the calamondin tree (*Citrus x macrocarpa*) in our in-floor planter. I styled the top of the soil with stones for a cleaner look and to keep Zoey from digging up the soil (this page). I keep the calamondin pruned so as not to block the path to the powder room door (opposite below). A sober gray planter allows this leafy *Goeppertia orbifolia* to be the star of the show (opposite above).

When I was plant styling my home and trying to find the perfect planters for every single plant, nothing could top our in-floor planter. Yes, you read that right. You see, sometimes good things can come out of bad situations. While we were renovating our home, inactive termite damage was found in the wood flooring of the living room. Not wanting the new floor there to clash with the original boards elsewhere, we decided to get new flooring for the entire downstairs of the house.

While this caused us a lot of stress, as well as lost time and money, a silver lining did appear. We were going to place a new window on the south side of the house, and I suggested we build an in-floor planter in front of it before we installed the new floor. Then we could plant a citrus tree, a calamondin (*Citrus* x *macrocarpa*) in it and have it growing out of the floor, just like in *Jack and the Beanstalk*. This would blur the line between indoors and out (if it hadn't been blurred already by the 300 other plants). "But how does it drain?" you may ask. Well, we had piping connected to a drain in the base of the planter that leads outside. You could say the house became the planter, and what a perfect one it is.

Even when you don't have a plant in mind, it's hard not to purchase a new planter when you see one you love, just in case it works for a future project. But when I'm styling my own space, I'll most likely choose the plant for a particular area first, then select the planter that it will be styled in. The in-floor planter was an exception to this rule.

Once I've figured out the light situation and decided on the type of plant, I consider the colors and textures of the pieces nearby and pick a planter that vibes well with the plant. You can choose either to mimic the texture or color of the plant or to create a cool conflict between the two. For example, the smooth, leathery foliage of a rubber tree (*Ficus elastica*) in a fluted terra-cotta planter feels like a perfect combination. Or imagine a Madagascar palm (*Pachypodium lamerei*) in a Japanese *nerikomi*-style planter. The coupling of the layers of colored clay with the thorny plant would be divine.

PERFECT PLANTERS 29

HOW TO FIND THE PERFECT PLANTER

There are many ways to go about finding the right planter. First things first, shop local. Check out your neighborhood plant shop to see what planters it has in stock. These could vary from luxury designer brands to the work of local makers, some of whom may also take commissions. There have been plenty of times when I've had a certain look in mind for a particular plant and found a local ceramicist to create the perfect planter. Just like having an outfit tailored, this may have a higher price tag attached, but it could be worth it if you're looking for something unique.

You could also make a day of it and visit all the thrift stores and vintage stores in your area. These are treasure troves of planters or vessels that can serve as planters. For example, a wooden bowl can be transformed into a pot in which to mount your staghorn fern (*Platycerium*).

If you're having a hard time finding what you're looking for locally, online stores have figured out ways to ship ceramics safely across the globe. And when shopping online, your options are endless. You'll have a choice from big-box stores to small boutiques and from ceramicists nearby to those who live thousands of miles away.

One question I get asked all the time is where to source larger planters. That can be a bit challenging, depending on where you live. I would recommend bigger design stores online or well-stocked local plant shops. Although many large planters look pretty basic, you can always paint or decorate them to give them a unique flair.

POTTED UP
This *nerikomi*-style vase by Fay Ray Clay is used to propagate a watermelon begonia cutting, while a textured glazed planter holds agave cuttings (above left and right). Opposite, clockwise from top left: an austral gem fern (*Asplenium dimorphum x difforme*) dressed in a glazed ceramic planter to keep the soil moist; an *Aglaonema* 'Silver Queen' styled in a simple terra-cotta planter on a metal stand; a terrarium styled in a fillable lamp; a Meyer lemon tree in a bold, face-shaped Mexican planter.

LIVING WALLS

The power of a vertical display of plants to transform a space and bring the outdoors in is just remarkable. Whether it's a built-in living wall with its own irrigation system or simply a wall styled with a selection of mounted plants, the "wow" factor is instant. The simple fact is that you're taking what is typically a flat, hard surface and making it literally come alive. With their added warmth, color, texture, and depth, plants provide a new meaning for the phrase "wall art," doing what wallpaper or a fine art painting can't do.

A living wall is an art piece that is forever changing, morphing, and becoming new. It's a continual work in progress and a breath of fresh air. Creating a vertical feature like this can set the tone for a room or even the entire home. Although finding the right vessels or foundation for your plants is important, it's the decisions on the types of plants you want to see growing out of the wall that will truly make it art. Does a particular flowering plant look nice next to a certain bushy plant? Or will the color of the blooms of that flowering plant clash beside the other colors in the room? All of this must be considered when styling a living wall.

Even the most ordinary home has a potted plant in the corner of a room or a few around the house, but to assign an area of the home to your plants, to have a wall with greenery growing from it, is making a statement. And clearly that statement is "I'm living wild!" I've been living this lifestyle for a while now and I treat the concept of living wild as if it's my default. It comes standard with the 2023 Hilton Carter model. With the trend of biophilic design being more popular now than ever, you'll see more and more homes, offices, and commercial spaces applying living art to their walls.

IRRIGATION SYSTEMS

In my plant shop, *green neighbor*, we wanted a living wall that wouldn't need to be connected to a drain or running water because we don't have a direct water line to the building. Creating a recirculating living wall was the best way of going about this because it only requires a tank that supplies water to the wall plants via pipes running along the sides and top of the wall. The water then recirculates and the tank only needs to be refilled weekly. This is the most common style of living wall that you'll see used in commercial spaces. In residential homes, they aren't as widely used because of the humidity they produce. Luckily, there are businesses offering more compact designs for smaller spaces and looks that are more modern, clean, and can fit in with your design aesthetic.

GREEN NEIGHBOR
Our living wall is one of the main features in my plant shop *green neighbor*. Using an irrigation system to cycle water through the wall means the plants potted in the felt pockets get all the moisture they need. Our mission is to inspire our customers to create a stylish space using plants.

WALL PLANTED

I've said it before and I'll say it again, sometimes when you run out of available floor space, you're forced to utilize the vertical space. When it comes to styling a space with plants, wall planters help you do just that. Like mounted plants, they can hold their own alone or with many planters arranged on the wall together. Just as your options for floor planters can feel endless, the pool of wall planters out there is deep. However, as I explained in *Perfect Planters* (see pages 26–31), making the decision on which planters work best for your aesthetic is important. Another thing to consider when designing a living wall of planters is that most of them don't have drainage holes, which means you'll have to be mindful of your watering and go the extra mile to tilt the planters over a sink from time to time to drain out any excess water.

LIVING ART
The Hilton Carter cove cradles are propagation vessels that I designed as a way of creating a living wall in a space that can't be irrigated. They also give the opportunity to produce more plants in style (above left and opposite). A ceramic wall planter from the Hilton Carter for Target collection (below).

PROPAGATION DOMINATION

When I first thought of creating a living wall in my home, I was living with my wife in an apartment where there wasn't much we could do to change the space. We definitely couldn't add an irrigation system and have plants growing from felt baskets on the wall. So, in considering other ways to create a living wall without altering the structure of the apartment, I decided to style the wall using vessels I had designed to propagate plant cuttings in water. This allowed me to have the look of lushness growing from the wall but would also allow me to get my security deposit back once we moved out.

To protect the wall from moisture damage, I used a water-resistant paint and stayed mindful of any vines looking to grow onto the wall. You can buy many types of wall-mounted vessels for propagation. The beauty in creating this style of living wall is that it not only helps you increase the number of plants you have in your home, but it gives you the ability to share a piece of your home with others, too. You can take a cutting from the wall and gift it to a friend, inspiring a passion for plants in someone else.

WALL COVERINGS

A bloom from a mounted *Tillandsia cyanea* adds a splash of color to our sunroom (above). To protect walls from moisture damage, I place felt pads on the backs of the mounted plants (right). A mounted white rabbit's foot fern (below). The mounted plants create a living wall effect in our sunroom (opposite).

MOUNTED MURALS

There is nothing like seeing a staghorn fern (*Platycerium*) mounted on a board and displayed on a gallery wall. Whether it's one single plant or an entire wall of them, it's a showstopper. Epiphytic plants that typically grow on trees in the wild are especially well suited to being mounted. The best options are orchids, air plants (*Tillandsia*), fishbone cacti (*Epiphyllum anguliger*), ferns, hoyas, bromeliads, and mosses.

Your mounting options are varied, too. You can mount these plants on pieces of perfectly cut cedar boards in nice frames or on pieces of reclaimed wood that have a live edge showing. You can cover the roots with cork or wrap them in sheet moss (*Hypnum curvifolium*) and sphagnum. After that, the eye for design is going to show itself in how you arrange the plants on the wall. The only downside to creating a living wall in this way is that mounted plants will need to be taken down once a week to be watered, unlike an irrigation or propagation wall that allows you to care for the plants right at the wall. But as they say, "nothing worth doing is easy."

CENTER-PIECES

Wanting to be the center of attention gets a bad rap. Why not show off your excellence and shine so that the world feels a bit brighter? That's exactly what a centerpiece does when styled in a home.

Centerpieces have always been particularly floral forward. A bouquet of cut stems that will eventually die tend to spring to mind when you think of a centerpiece. They take center stage on coffee tables and dining room buffets, entryway consoles, and kitchen islands, adding a sculptural moment and pop of color.

While I love a floral bouquet and what it can bring to a table setting, as a plant stylist my goal is to find ways to introduce living greenery into the home. So instead of replacing bouquet after bouquet as they wither away and die, why not find the right plant, dress it in the perfect planter, and style it in the center of your table? That way, you'll still have a centerpiece bringing color and interest to your table, but one that will continue to grow and become one with the space. I, for one, am in love with the look and feel of sitting at a table and having the foliage of a plant on the table canopy over me. If that's not bringing the outdoors in, I'm not sure what is.

Depending on the available space on your table or countertop and the amount of light, your options are varied. If you're into the idea of a floral centerpiece, plants like *Anthurium* and *Alocasia* are ideal. We often tend to style a table setting for a particular occasion, one with a specific color palette, so purchasing fresh flowers may seem like the best option. But exactly the same ideas can be put into practice with your potted plants.

Let's say the occasion is a summer party. You could position a Meyer lemon tree (*Citrus* x *limon* 'Meyer') in the center of your island or table and pick lemons from the tree to use in the cocktails you're serving guests. If you're having an intimate dinner with friends, styling

MAIN COURSE
A centerpiece created from plant cuttings and purchased bird of paradise stems stays bright and colorful longer than a bouquet and the cuttings will develop roots, allowing them to be propagated (opposite). This *Philodendron* 'Birkin' centerpiece matches the striped placemats (above left). An energetic rubber tree setting the mood (above).

TABLE DRESSING

I styled a Japanese aralia in a spotted clay planter in the center of interior designer Stephanie Bradshaw's kitchen table. I love the way it looks under the wicker pendant and how the cheetah print pops against the walls (below). On our kitchen island, I used a large Australian tree fern as a centerpiece and statement plant. The fronds unfurl high above the room, creating a shelter for those sitting under it (right). In the kitchen of activist Tarana J. Burke, a red anthurium in a glazed terra-cotta planter brings a pop of color (opposite).

plants that sit low to the table, like a grouping of succulents, will add a touch of greenery and allow conversation to flow easily without blocking anyone's view. If planning a fun, informal brunch, you could take cuttings from your plants and arrange a propagation centerpiece. Not only will this look beautiful, but the plants will eventually develop roots and you can pot them in soil to create new plants (See my book *Wild Creations* for how to create centerpiece cuttings).

Finally, you could bring in a floral element by taking cuttings from plants that have recently bloomed, such as begonias, peperomias or orchid cacti (*Epiphyllum*), and place them in your chosen vessel.

A living centerpiece can change the entire mood of a room and attract the attention it rightfully deserves.

STATEMENT PLANTS

When designing your home, or even just one room, a good starting point is to ask yourself what kind of statement you are hoping to make with the space. Perhaps you're a lover of color and envision a bold color-block mural painted on one wall? Or a minimalist, in which case clean lines and muted tones give you life. But whatever that statement is, it will be evident as soon as you enter the room.

Within that larger statement sit further statement pieces. For example, a grand piano placed in the middle of the room would be a statement piece. Or an original Kerry James Marshall painting hanging on the wall. In exactly the same way, when it comes to plant styling an interior, you'll want to add some statement plants. But what defines a "statement"? Well, a plant isn't labeled a statement plant based purely on its size but because of the detail that it brings to a room. It could be a statement thanks to its vibrant colors, the intricate patterns on the leaves, the shape and/or texture of the foliage, or the pattern of growth. A 2-ft/60-cm *Ficus* bonsai (such as *Ficus retusa*) can be just as eye-catching as a 12-ft/3.6-m rubber tree (*Ficus elastica*). Like the Marshall painting, it's a conversation starter, a tone setter.

But—let's be real—often a statement plant will be on the larger side. That's because a large plant can instantly create a "wow" factor, bringing drama and a touch of the outdoors to an interior. If you place that 12-ft/3.6-m rubber tree in a corner of the living room or in the entryway, its impact is instant and its beauty can be admired from a distance. But to admire the bonsai, you'll need to get a touch closer. While both will make a statement, it's easier and more immediate with the larger plant.

WELCOMING MOMENTS
In the home of interior designer, Stephanie Bradshaw, I styled a large *Ficus binnendijkii 'Alii'* in a ribbed planter as a beautiful "welcome" moment in the entryway (right). In the kitchen of artists Evan Guidera and Fay Ray, I styled a *Ficus benjamina* 'Danielle' to add a pop of green against the white (opposite left). A thriving lady palm sets the tone in the kitchen of Shawn and Anne Chopra (opposite right).

BIG PLANT ENERGY
Seen from a different angle, the *Ficus binnendijkii 'Alii'* in Stephanie Bradshaw's entryway makes a bold impact. A mounted staghorn fern outside our home (opposite above left). In John Makowski and Bridget Weininger's home, I styled a *Ficus lyrata* to sit high in the room (opposite above right). Fan palms can make any space feel tropical (opposite below right).

I like to say that it only takes a single plant to change the atmosphere in a room. While my particular aesthetic is what some might describe as "all green everything," I like styling minimalist spaces with one large pop of greenery. There's something so calming about a single tree in a room. When you're limiting the number of pieces in a space, it's important to be selective. You need to tell yourself, "I'm choosing this particular plant because of XYZ." Let your theme or inspiration lead you in your decision making.

For example, if the theme for my living room was "Mexican loft," I'd choose a ponytail palm (*Beaucarnea recurvata*) or a large fan palm (*Chamaerops humilis*). They are both native to Mexico and have a sculptural look that would complement concrete, tile, and exposed metals. If the theme for my dining room was "Parisian Chic," I'd style a large tree fern (*Dicksonia antarctica*) in a tall pot in a corner of the room or as a centerpiece so that the fronds could form a canopy over those that dined under it. Whatever your theme, a statement plant brings it to life.

You might choose to have a few statement plants in just one room or dot them throughout your home. Choosing and sourcing them is part of what makes the collecting of houseplants more personal, special, and fun. There is now a method behind the lushness.

PERFECT STATEMENT PLANTS

Five interior design styles and the perfect statement plants for them:

MINIMALIST
Olive (*Olea europaea*)

An olive tree works perfectly in a minimalist space, thanks to its small and delicate silvery green leaves, which are simple in their design and sit perfectly against the neutral color palette of homes decorated in this style.

MODERN
Bird of paradise (*Strelitzia*)

The bird of paradise is a large tropical plant that has broad, sleek, paddle-shaped foliage and vibrant flowers. It complements the clean lines and simple color palette of modern design.

BOHO CHIC
Fiddle-leaf fig (*Ficus lyrata*)

The ever-trendy fiddle-leaf fig has made its way into many interiors, but for me it fits best in a boho chic room, where its glossy dark green leaves and elegant stance can add to the quirky, playful vibe associated with this style.

INDUSTRIAL
Candelabra tree (*Euphorbia ingens*)

The sculptural shape and simple green lines of the candelabra tree make it the perfect partner for an industrial or loft-style interior, which is typically made up of raw materials, exposed metal beams, brick walls, and straight lines.

SCANDINAVIAN
Banyan (*Ficus benghalensis* 'Audrey')

The clean, off-white trunk and branches and large, glossy oval leaves of the banyan would work great in a Scandi-styled space that aims for simplicity in form, color, and texture.

OH SO QUIET
A majestic Australian tree fern sits on top of a pedestal to make its presence felt (above). One of my favorite things to consider is the way in which a plant's foliage develops and Australian tree ferns fronds are just so calming to watch unfurl. I styled a towering *Ficus lyrata* in the bedroom of my studio to make a loud statement in this quiet space (opposite).

THE ART OF THE PEDESTAL

Have you ever heard the saying "one person's trash is another person's treasure"? That's kind of how I feel about plant stands. To me, one person's side table is another person's plant stand. But in all honesty, doesn't every surface have the potential to become a plant stand? Whether it's a side table, a stool, an old chair, a countertop, a coffee table, or a shelf, these are all surfaces on which you can display plants like living art. That's why I think I'm over the term "plant stand." I believe it's about time that we elevate (pun intended) the way we see the plant stand and give it the recognition it deserves. The plant stand as you've previously known it is now the pedestal.

When you think about what a pedestal is and what it represents, its main function is to lift a work of art higher in a room, giving the viewer the opportunity to take in the full beauty of the piece. First devised in ancient times to support statues, columns, and other art, they did a lot of heavy lifting (OK, at this point, just know that all puns are intended). In a gallery setting, most pedestals are designed to fade into the background and are often painted to match the walls. The curator wants the pedestal to disappear so that the art is the only thing you see. At home, however, the pedestal is meant to be seen. Like the walnut chairs you meticulously picked out to pair perfectly with your dining table or the armoire that you placed in your living room because you knew it would highlight the sconces on the wall, the pedestals that become a part of your home design should attract attention.

Fortunately, the options are plentiful. There are so many well-designed structures on which you can place your plants to give your home an extra touch of creativity. Designed with purpose and character, they stand out on their own.

HIGH PROFILE
There is a real art to styling a plant on a pedestal—it puts emphasis on the plant, the planter, and, of course, the pedestal. The pedestal's height, color, and material are all deciding factors when it comes to deciding on the type of plant you'll want to style on top and the impact it has in the room.

You can find pedestals made from so many different materials, in various heights, and in a spectrum of styles. Some planters are now designed to have pedestals attached to them so that they work together as one. As an artist and a plant stylist, I like to marry those worlds together. Why can't one pedestal hold a small sculpture, while across the room another supports a gorgeous *Anthurium regale*? There's a sense of artistry in this arrangement that is delicate but impactful.

I look to find as many unique ways as possible to introduce a pedestal into a room. Plant styling is all about understanding where to place a plant so that it has the greatest visual impact while being considerate of its needs. A pedestal can present a plant in a different light, both literally and metaphorically. For instance, you'll notice that I tend to use taller pedestals in corners to give height to plants that would typically sit lower in a room. This adjustment takes that plant from being part of the background noise to a focal point in the room.

My desire is for everyone to see plants as living art. Unlike your traditional art forms, plants are always a work in progress. They are forever shapeshifting, changing, and evolving into something new. That means your home, and you, will always be in a state of flux. And that, to me, is the beauty of life itself.

GOLDEN OPPORTUNITIES
I styled a Ming aralia on a pedestal here because it will grow vertically without blocking the sunroom door (this page). A snake plant on a chunky wood pedestal (opposite above left). A *Ficus triangularis* has been lifted up out of the way on the stairwell (opposite above right). A *Philodendron* 'Rojo Congo' is raised up high to make it easier to admire (opposite below).

OUTDOOR GLAMOUR

I've spoken a lot about bringing the outdoors in, but there are times of the year—spring, summer, and parts of fall, depending on where you live—that you can keep the outdoors...outdoors. Basically, what I'm saying is that our indoor plants can also take a much-needed summer vacation.

Indoors, we work hard to recreate the climate that our plants need to thrive by providing them with humidifiers and misting them weekly. Thankfully, when the seasons change and it gets a little warmer outside, we get to take a break and allow the outdoor elements to do the heavy lifting. But what nature can't do is arrange our plants and planters around the exterior of our homes in a way that is stylish and practical. That, my friends, is up to you.

Before you move your plants outside, you'll need to slowly acclimatize them to the elements by bringing them outside for a few hours under shade and then back indoors overnight, repeating this process for at least two to three days and gradually extending the amount of time they spend outdoors. Once you've checked the weather and made certain that the temperature will remain above 50°F/10°C at night (and some houseplants can tolerate periods of lower temperatures), then you can have fun styling them around the exterior of your home.

Just as bringing tropical plants indoors can transform your home into an exotic destination, the same goes for styling plants outside. If you live in a mid-century modern home in Chicago but want to feel as if you're in Pasadena, California, during the summer, you can style sago palms (*Cycas revoluta*) and fan palms (*Chamaerops humilis*) on your terrace or veranda. If your look is more desert than tropical, more Arizona than Peru, you can style cacti and succulents around your outdoor space and your home will look just like the area you're trying to recreate.

The style of your home is one thing to consider, but take note of the local climate too. For example, if you live somewhere that gets a lot of rain during spring and summer, you're not going to be successful using desert plants outside. By the same token, a fern-heavy look that requires high humidity is not going to work in an arid climate. Sometimes you have to work inside of the box to make sure the plants that you've moved outdoors for the season return alive and healthy when fall/winter comes.

HOME GROWN
The silhouette of our home attracted us to it from the very start. Being able to add tropical greenery around it was the dream (opposite and above). Outside the home of Irena Stein, I styled a grouping of plants that love indirect light (above left).

As someone who has lived most of his life in an apartment without access to an outdoor space like a terrace, patio, or deck, when my wife and I purchased a home it was of utmost importance that we had an outdoor space to turn into a beautiful garden. Fortunately for us, we were able to purchase an American Colonial-style home, built in 1905, with alluring surroundings. Tucked between evergreens, it felt quaint, and I knew it was a home we needed to claim as our own.

As a lover of tropical plants, I knew that I would gravitate toward them when I had the opportunity to create a garden of my own. During my time in California, I was always drawn to homes surrounded by a cluster of large palm trees. So when it came to styling the front of our home, which faces north, I went with a large spindle palm (*Hyophorbe verschaffeltii*) as our statement plant (see pages 42–47). I dressed it in an off-white planter in the style of our home, so it looked as if it had been growing there long before we arrived. I surrounded the palm with other tropicals, including a *Philodendron bernardopazii*, *P. xanadu*, an Australian tree fern (*Dicksonia antarctica*), and many others to make our home in Baltimore, Maryland, feel like you might need your passport to get here.

The east side of our home, which gets plenty of morning sun, is where I styled my collection of small and medium cacti and succulents, creating my own private Oaxaca desert. With these desert plants styled in porous pots of all shapes and sizes, this area has a very different look and feel from the north side of the house.

LIKE-MINDED INDIVIDUALS
A styling concept I love to utilize is creating groupings. Here I've styled a group of cacti and succulents together to create a "desert" moment on the east side of our home.

54 DESIGNING A LIVING HOME

BLURRED LINES
Having a deck to enjoy during the warmer months expands the space you have for indoor/outdoor living (opposite). Blurring the line between indoor and out is easier when we're able to fold the accordion doors back and create one large room (right). Another grouping of plants—these specimens love full sun during the spring and summer (below right).

Lastly, when it came to the south side of our home, which is sun-kissed all day long, plant styling our deck with sun-loving specimens was a must. When taking your indoor plants outside, never place a plant that prefers low light levels somewhere that gets direct sun from the south and west. That will be the death of that plant. To keep the look clean and consistent, all the plants on the deck are in terra-cotta planters. I layered a grouping of plants on the right corner, so as not to block the path to the staircase.

Unlike the eastern side of the house, where we don't have a lot of foot traffic, here on the deck we do. During spring, summer, and fall, it's a lively space for hosting parties, for quiet mornings with a cup of coffee, and downtime with the family. If you're styling cacti in high-traffic areas like this, be mindful to work in thornless plants. Here, I've used a large pencil cactus (*Euphorbia tirucalli*), a large standard spineless prickly pear and small variegated prickly pear cactus (both varieties of *Opuntia ellisiana*) and a *Euphorbia ingens*. I also added a few other sun-lovers, like a ponytail palm (*Beaucarnea recurvata*), sago palm (*Cycas revoluta*), and gold dust croton (*Codiaeum variegatum* 'Gold Dust').

On the left side of the deck, I positioned a large majestic palm (*Ravenea rivularis*) to balance out the other plants and hide the umbrella stand. On the table top, I styled a *Caladium lindenii* 'Magnificum' in a white clay planter. Its patterned foliage works so well with the striped umbrella.

When styling the exterior of a client's home, I use exactly the same strategies and techniques to ensure not only that the plants thrive in their new outdoor locations but also that they're able to move back indoors safely at the end of summer.

TIPS FOR PLANT STYLING OUTDOORS

Make sure you're aware of the weather forecast and what the temperature highs and lows will be. A low of above 50°F/10°C at night is necessary before you move your plants outside.

Acclimatize plants slowly by bringing them outdoors under a shaded area for a few hours and then back inside for a few hours, repeating this step for two to three days before leaving them outdoors for the season.

The type of light your plants require indoors will still be the case outdoors. If your houseplants thrive in bright, indirect light, placing them in dappled or lightly shaded areas will be perfect. Any north-facing area of your exterior will work.

If you have direct-sun-loving plants like cacti, succulents, ponytail palms (*Beaucarnea recurvata*), or crotons, you'll want to gradually relocate them to sunny outdoor spots. Try placing them on the eastern side of the house for a week or so before moving them to the south or west side of your home for the rest of the season.

Beware of local wildlife that might like the taste of your houseplants. Plants like *Calathea* and *Alocasia* are tempting snacks for rabbits and deer.

If you've purchased a plant during spring or summer and have kept it outside all season, make sure to have a plan for its position once it has to come indoors.

PATIO PRINCIPLES
A detail of the plants I styled outside the home of designer Jamie Campbell and artist Drury Bynum (above right). The patio should be treated like an extension of the home, so I styled Jamie and Drury's with additional plants, lanterns, and pillows, to make a spring evening feel a little warmer (opposite). On their patio table, the centerpiece is a Song of India (*Dracaena reflexa*) and a *Peperomia obtusifolia* (right).

GREENHOUSE GOODNESS
On the side of the gorgeous home of Barbara Voss is a little greenhouse that will make any plant lover jealous (right). While Barbara usually uses the greenhouse to shelter her outdoor plants, here I've styled it for a little party—I filled the perimeter of the room with plants and hung staghorn ferns from above, then, with the help of stylist Jamie Campbell, prepared the table for a party. A grouping of succulents in one corner (below).

TIPS FOR BRINGING YOUR PLANTS BACK INDOORS

Place the plant in its planter in a vessel that's large enough to hold the entire planter. Fill the vessel to the top with lukewarm water. Let the plant sit there for 10 to 15 minutes, washing out or killing any pests that might be in the soil.

During that time, take a damp cloth and wipe the foliage down, removing any pests, dirt, or debris. Once the 15 minutes are up, remove the plant and planter from the vessel and allow the soil to drain out for a few hours before bringing it indoors.

Once you're ready to bring the plant back inside, again you will have to slowly acclimatize it to its indoor spot, first placing it somewhere that enjoys almost as much light as the plant was receiving outdoors. Leave the plant there for a week, and then move it to the spot where you want to style it. However, if the plant is going to end up in a low-light location, you will have to transfer it to a medium-light spot a week after bringing it inside, and then a week later move it to the low-light area. This will help the plant transition back into its usual home without causing too much fuss.

DESIGNER PLANTS

TEN HIGH-PROFILE PLANTS THAT REFLECT THE COLORS, TEXTURES AND PATTERNS OF THE HOME.

I know, I know. I can hear you all saying it out loud to yourselves right now, "Designer plants?! What the what?!" But hear me out. As an interior and plant stylist, I know that bringing out the best in your clients' spaces requires a great sense of color and a feel for texture. But having an eye for design goes beyond just bringing together inanimate objects. That eye also sees how to mix living flora seamlessly into a space. You also have to be tapped into what brings the "wow." You're not only following trends but setting them. Just as an interior designer would take the time to consider carefully how the solidity of a concrete dining table could tie in well with the soft, warm texture of red leather chairs, or how the bright pops of color in a piece of art can connect with a few throw pillows across the room, that same thought process and energy can be applied to plant styling.

As I've mentioned earlier, when I plant style a space, I always let the light lead me. Knowing the quality of the natural light you have coming into a room will guide you in understanding the types of plants that can thrive in the space. Once you have that knowledge, "the world is your oyster." Ok, maybe not your oyster. More like, "the world is your plant store where you can now have access to all the plants that can tolerate low-light situations." Basically, that's when the fun starts. You're now able to introduce plants into a space and play with how their color scheme brings out the pattern of the wallpaper or how the texture or shape of the foliage can be reminiscent of the texture or shape of the couch. It goes beyond just bringing plants into a space to blur the line between the indoors and outdoors—it starts a conversation of life truly imitating art and vice versa.

In this chapter I will share a few of my favorite designer plants and show you how to look at them in a different light when designing a space. I believe we should not purchase that new rug or coffee table without considering the plant we intend to place on top of it. My hope is that you leave this chapter with renewed excitement for bringing the best out in your life with plants and your world at home.

1 BEGONIA 'ARGENTEO-GUTTATA'

I know what you've been asking yourself. "What is the name of that fabric that looks like a bowl of Cream of Wheat?" Yeah, I know—you've seen it everywhere and on every piece of furniture that designers could possibly wrap it in. From beautiful, bulbous modern couches to curvy accent chairs and throw pillows, this fabric has taken over. In interior design, there is no other fabric more trendy, more "IT" than bouclé, which comes from the French word *boucler*, meaning "to curl." I'm sure they're referring to the way the yarn curls, but I can only see it as "curl up," as in "let's curl up on our bouclé couch." Or let's at least snuggle it like a child snuggles its lovey or blankie. Bouclé furniture is beloved by interior designers. Its soft look is what makes it so attractive. With so many of us bringing this hip fabric into our homes, it seems we are all looking to add a little softness as a foil to the straight lines and hard surfaces of other furnishings. As I've said many times before, the addition of plants can have a similar effect. So as a plant stylist, I'd be remiss if I didn't recommend the perfect plant to complement your bouclé-swaddled piece of decor.

Drumroll, please! The crowd quiets, the lights dim, and a spotlight hits the center of the curtain (oh, the sweet, sweet drama). It is with great pleasure that I introduce you to the *Begonia* 'Argenteo-guttata'. The curtains part, and behind them…heaven. Ok, that's a little too dramatic. But it is a heavenly plant. They don't call it the angel-wing begonia for nothing. This is the Argenteo's world. We're just paying rent in it. Or maybe we're only subletting. Whenever I look at this plant, I see the beauty of bouclé staring back at me. Each leaf is in the shape of an angel's wing and covered in the same nubby texture as bouclé. But instead of being a creamy white color, it's silvery white with a dark green base and contoured in crimson. With beautiful pink blooms that unfurl throughout the year, it's no wonder it's so sought after. If bouclé is the "IT" fabric then the 'Argenteo-guttata' is the "IT" plant. Their connection in texture is one reason to style them together, but it's their standout capabilities that help them pull a room together.

STYLING TIP Just like the curvy furniture that suits bouclé fabric so well, a nice, curvy off-white glazed ceramic planter would be perfect for your 'Argenteo-guttata'. Placing it on a pedestal to give it some height in the room and to emphasize its angelic beauty is a must.

LIGHT Bright indirect light is going to provide the best growth and help the plant to bloom throughout the year. Put it in an east- or south-facing window where it can get dappled sun.

WATER Keep the soil evenly moist but not damp. Use a moisture meter to help gauge the moisture level. Once the top half of the soil feels dry, add some lukewarm water. This plant likes humidity, so adding a humidifier nearby would be beneficial.

> THIS IS THE ARGENTEO'S WORLD. WE'RE JUST PAYING RENT IN IT. OR MAYBE WE'RE ONLY SUBLETTING.

SOIL Wrap the roots in a soil medium that is well aerated with a mix of bark, sphagnum moss, a bit of perlite, and organic potting soil. This will help keep the soil moist for longer and help your plant thrive.

TEMPERATURE Style this plant in areas of your home that remain between 65–80°F/18–27°C during the day and no cooler than 60°F/16°C at night. Make sure to keep it away from the direct blast of air conditioners and heaters.

2 MONSTERA DELICIOSA 'ALBO VARIEGATA'

For centuries, marble has appeared in furniture design as a sign of luxury and wealth. While the cost of rare Victorian pieces may not be within your reach, many stores offer furniture made from marble. It's as popular now as it's ever been. But when marble tables and marbled plants cost the same amount of money, you know we have hit a new level of "designer" plants. The time is coming when plant shops will have security guards in them, like the Gucci store. Honestly, I wouldn't be surprised if in a few years a luxury brand like Gucci opened a plant shop or launched a collection of planters and plant care accessories.

Although I think the idea that some plants are more "valuable" than others can cause those who own these plants to be neglectful of their less-expensive plants, I can see why someone would have the urge to purchase a $2,000 *Monstera deliciosa* 'Albo Variegata'. I mean, have you seen this plant? Yes, I know, there are images right here in front of you, but have you really seen it, IRL? Its foliage has the glamour and color unpredictability of that first pour of milk melting into the darkness of a cup of black coffee and the astonishment of when the front end of an okapi meets up with the back end of an okapi. Help me figure this out, because I don't understand what happened here. Did someone just dip a deer's butt in zebra print? That's the sort of surprise you feel when you first see the Albo.

With its variegated pattern spreading across each leaf, the Albo reminds me of the marble surfaces that are so effective when styled indoors. So, whether I look to place one in the same room as a marble table, piece of decor, or pedestal, I want that connection to be understood and recognized. In interior design, you're connecting the entire world of each room. One piece here speaks to another piece there, and so on. If I was looking to place my marble coffee table next to a leather settee with gold legs, I'd emphasize that same connection by possibly placing the Albo in a gold planter. Alternatively, if I were looking to add a touch of drama, I might style the Albo on a black terrazzo table in order to have the competing patterns go head to head. The true power and beauty in all this is the relationship between a soft, organic form and the hard, inanimate objects in a space. Regardless of its monetary cost, the value of this plant within your interior design is priceless.

> THE TRUE POWER AND BEAUTY IN ALL THIS IS THE RELATIONSHIP BETWEEN A SOFT, ORGANIC FORM AND THE HARD, INANIMATE OBJECTS IN A SPACE.

STYLING TIP Do yourself a favor and style the Albo in a safe or behind bulletproof glass. I'm just kidding, but honestly, place it where it can be showcased and admired. I recommend styling it in a porous vessel made of concrete or terra-cotta.

LIGHT Find a place that gets bright indirect light for best results. The brighter the light, the bigger the foliage will be, but avoid placing your Albo in direct sun. A spot below a skylight or directly in an east- or north-facing window would be perfect.

WATER Water once the top half of the soil is dry and then water deeply. This plant loves humid climates, so add a humidifier or mist once a week.

SOIL Use a soil medium that is free-draining and loose, made with a mixture of perlite, peat moss, and organic potting soil.

TEMPERATURE The Albo is used to warm climates in the wild, so replicating that sort of feeling as much as you can indoors is only going to help yours flourish. Keep it in an area of the home that's kept at 65–75°F/18–24°C during the day and no cooler than 60°F/16°C at night.

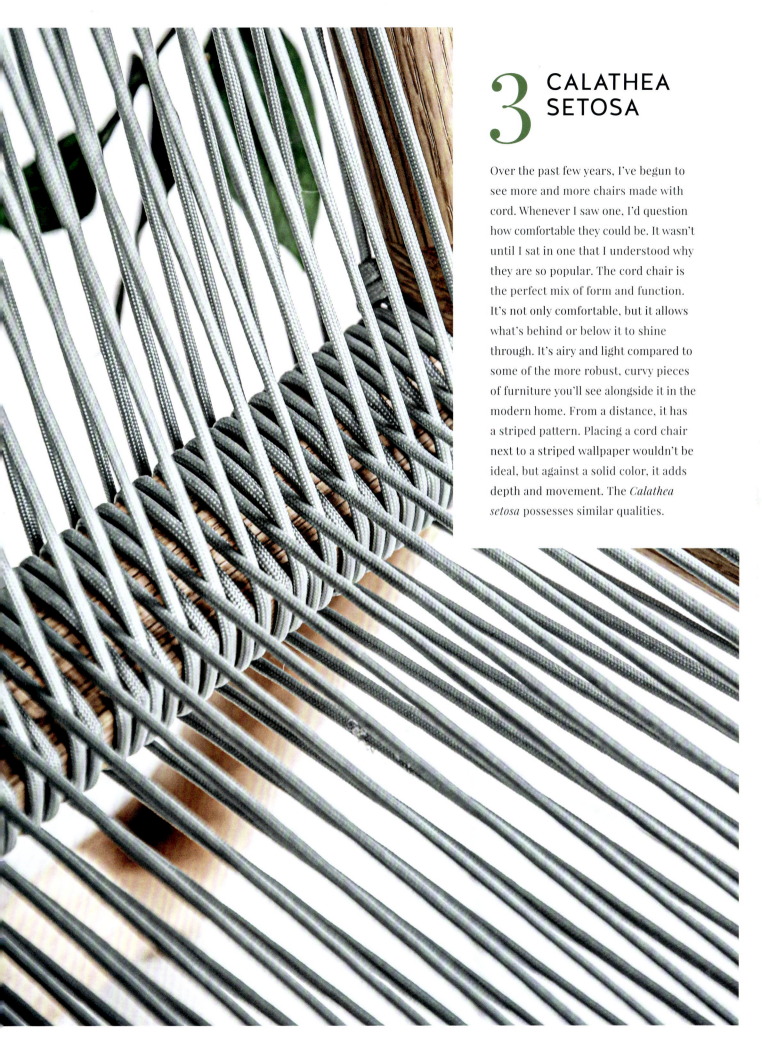

3 CALATHEA SETOSA

Over the past few years, I've begun to see more and more chairs made with cord. Whenever I saw one, I'd question how comfortable they could be. It wasn't until I sat in one that I understood why they are so popular. The cord chair is the perfect mix of form and function. It's not only comfortable, but it allows what's behind or below it to shine through. It's airy and light compared to some of the more robust, curvy pieces of furniture you'll see alongside it in the modern home. From a distance, it has a striped pattern. Placing a cord chair next to a striped wallpaper wouldn't be ideal, but against a solid color, it adds depth and movement. The *Calathea setosa* possesses similar qualities.

As with all calatheas, the colors and patterns of *C. setosa*'s foliage are what many of us find so captivating. The upper side of each leaf shows off deep green stripes on a muted green background, while the underside presents the typical calathea maroon hue. Good looks aside, one of the most loved qualities of Calatheas is the way they "dance" throughout the day. While this isn't something you can view in real time, time-lapse photography reveals how the foliage moves up and down and the leaves fold together like hands in prayer, giving calatheas the nickname "prayer plants." Their bold stripes make them perfect for styling in minimalistic spaces or against more solid patterns.

If there is a cord chair in the room, you bet I would want to style a *C. setosa* on the other side of the room to counterbalance it. The same goes for other striped patterns. It's trendy to mix stripes of varying thicknesses, so placing a Setosa next to a thick striped wallpaper would be brilliant. Or try placing it in a room with artwork that brings out the lines in the plant and vice versa. When it comes to the *C. setosa*, it's not only the leaves that play a role in how you style it, but also its long red stems.

> ONE OF THE MOST LOVED QUALITIES OF CALATHEAS IS THE WAY THEY DANCE THROUGHOUT THE DAY.

STYLING TIP Place your *Calathea setosa* in a pot that complements its stripes and leaf size. With the stems reaching out far when the leaves are open, a low, wide pot would be perfect.

LIGHT Style in a spot that gets bright indirect to medium light. While this plant can tolerate various types of light exposure, the brighter the light, the better it is for promoting growth and vibrancy. Avoid direct sun.

WATER Try to keep the soil moist but not wet. Water once the top inch/ 2.5cm of soil is dry to the touch. When the *C. setosa* is too dry, you will see the leaves start to curl. It's best to water the plant on a regular basis to prevent this from occurring. Placing a humidifier in the room will help with the moisture level.

SOIL Make sure the roots are wrapped in a soil medium that is well aerated with a mix of bark, sphagnum moss, and organic potting soil. This will keep the soil moist for longer and help your plant thrive.

TEMPERATURE For best results, keep this plant in an area of your home that stays at 60–75°F/16–24°C.

4 PHILODENDRON BRANDTIANUM

Some call her Brandtianum, others call her Brandy. Just don't call her basic. The *Philodendron brandtianum* is as designer as designer plants can get. If she had her way, she'd live in a Tiffany diamond-encrusted hanging basket with a Birkin clutched to her—not the bag, but her cousin the *P.* 'Birkin'. She's highbrow, but not high maintenance. She needs light but IS light. She puts the "ATE" in "dominate." She's THAT plant.

So, when brought into your home, the Brandtianum has to be styled correctly, with intention. Her allure comes from the silky, silvery, heart-shaped foliage, which glides gracefully along lean vines. The silvery swirl pattern that wraps itself around the greens in the leaf is reminiscent of wood fibers that form organic lines in a piece of timber. When you think about it, this makes a lot of sense. Nature has a way of replicating itself.

So, when it comes to plant styling, the Brandtianum can add wood-grain texture and appearance where there is none, possibly making a connection to a piece of wooden furniture across the room. In our home, where there are many pieces of furniture and decor made from wood, I like to place a Brandtianum in corners and pockets where its foliage can stand out against a white wall or another solid surface. The connection between a plant and a particular object in the room guides the eye from one spot to another throughout the space, whether you are aware of it or not. That's one of the signs of a well-designed home.

Just as you might search for the perfect way to transition a particular hardwood flooring into a ceramic tiled floor, you can find inspiration there to help you take the same considerations into account when it comes to the type of materials with which you surround your plant. The Brandtianum looks great when paired with marble, gold, concrete, and any other natural material. So whether you're looking to style her in a pot made of one of these materials or on top of them, you're making a wise choice.

THE CONNECTION BETWEEN A PLANT AND A PARTICULAR OBJECT IN THE ROOM GUIDES THE EYE FROM ONE SPOT TO ANOTHER THROUGHOUT THE SPACE.

STYLING TIP With the Brandtianum being a vine plant, it can be styled in a hanging pot or grown vertically in a floor planter supported by a wooden or moss-covered pole.

LIGHT Find a place that gets bright indirect to medium light. The brighter the light, the bigger the foliage will be, but avoid direct sun.

WATER Water deeply once the top half of the soil is dry. Adding a humidifier or misting once a week is helpful.

SOIL Use a soil medium that is free-draining and loose, made with a mixture of perlite, peat moss, and organic potting soil.

TEMPERATURE Style this plant in areas of your home that stay at 60–80°F/16–27°C, avoiding any direct drafts from air conditioners and heaters.

5
ALOCASIA CUPREA

Why didn't I title this part of the book "Fashion Plants"? I definitely dropped the ball here, because everyone would agree that when you look at the *Alocasia cuprea*, the first thing you see is a puffy jacket. And I don't mean a Diddy and Mase puffy jacket, I'm talking about the kind that resembles a pack of hotdogs and is super trendy during the fall and winter seasons. Perhaps I could even have written "Fashion" with a "PH": "Phashion Plants". There…I fixed it. Anyway, a neurologist would probably say this plant looks like a brain. Or an interior designer might say it looks like a metallic, fluted table. And since this a book is about interiors and styling, let's run with the latter. The word *cuprea* even means "copper" in Latin. Unlike me, and the title of this chapter, whoever named *A. cuprea* got it right.

The craze for fluted tables and chairs is real. I even chose it as a design element in one of the plant stands for my first Target collection. The aesthetic is clean and weighted, making it popular in modern, design-led homes. So when I'm plant styling a space and I notice that there is a fluted piece in the room, I like to add an *A. cuprea* to complement it and draw the eye from one side of the room to the other.

Although the plant's fluted foliage is organic, it shimmers like copper in the light that dances across its grooves. Its sheen plays really well with other metallic accents in a room, so it's a great choice for lofts and industrial warehouse spaces. As it's still on trend to match soft fabrics with hard metals, it should be easy to find a place to style this plant in most homes. *Alocasia cuprea* is a rare plant, so even though its name means copper, it should be treated like gold.

STYLING TIP Place your *Alocasia cuprea* in a pot with a great pattern or texture that will look nice next to its foliage. While I like seeing its leaves peeking out from a group of other tropical plants, it's also a good look to style it as a centerpiece on a table or on top of a pedestal to give it a little moment of its own.

LIGHT This plant needs a spot that receives ample amounts of bright indirect light. A north- or east-facing room, close to a window, would be ideal. Remember to keep it out of the reach of direct sun, however, as this can burn the foliage.

WATER Water with rain or distilled water whenever the top inch/2.5cm of soil is dry. The goal should be to keep the soil evenly moist but not wet. This plant thrives in humid conditions, so it helps to place it near a humidifier and mist once a week.

SOIL Make sure the roots are wrapped in a soil medium that is well aerated with a mix of bark, sphagnum moss, and organic potting soil. Refresh the soil once a year for best results.

TEMPERATURE Keep your *A. cuprea* in an area of your home that stays at 60–75°F/16–24°C.

> ALTHOUGH THE PLANT'S FLUTED FOLIAGE IS ORGANIC, IT SHIMMERS LIKE COPPER IN THE LIGHT THAT DANCES ACROSS ITS GROOVES.

6 ANTHURIUM REGALE

Sometimes when I watch my daughter taste or touch something for the very first time, I get a little envious. To have every part of your world be a brand-new experience must be incredible. I observe her as she digs her hands into soil or as she watches cold watermelon juice trickle down her arm after she takes a bite, or as we wrap her in soft fabrics to keep her warm and comfortable. The way her attention focuses on the thing she is touching and how her eyes light up with a million questions is a beautiful thing to witness. And when you're able to experience life like that as an adult, enjoying things as if for the first time, life tastes so sweet and rich. Do we all just want to be babies again?

When I was young, everything that was considered "quality" or "luxurious" in our home was covered in a protective layer of plastic. No one seemed to enjoy the furniture, which had been brought into the house as a source of comfort but more so as a statement of status. Back then, you wanted to keep nice things nice, even if it meant you couldn't enjoy them to the full. You might purchase a couch for your living room or a chair for your dining room but never experience what the fabric felt like against your skin.

At some point, things started to shift and the idea of enjoying the comfortable things in life became trendy. And I am so glad it did. Our most beloved pieces of furniture are made with some of the softest materials out there. I still remember the first time I experienced the feeling of velvet. It's a remarkable texture. There's a reason why everything that is described as velvety is often also described as rich or decadent, as if it's almost sinful to touch. Well, that's how I felt when I first brushed my fingertips across the surface of an *Anthurium regale* leaf.

Even the name *Anthurium regale* just sounds so fancy and so grandiose. I mean, honestly, why not just drop the second "e" and call it exactly what it is—regal. With its velvety green foliage and electric white veins, this exquisite specimen is one plant that your favorite plant lover's plant lover has in their collection. It's a rare beauty that many find difficult to bring indoors, but when given the proper care, it can be the perfect plant to style within your interior design. Its soft texture pairs perfectly with or against so many textures in the home. Personally, I like to combine it with hard, cold materials such as stone or clay for a pleasing juxtaposition.

Undoubtedly a statement plant, an *A. regale* in the home speaks to one's taste for the finer things in life. It's like seeing a piece designed by Kelly Wearstler or a ceramic by Magdalene Odundo in someone's living room—you know immediately what their taste level is. If this was 50 years ago, my grandmother would probably have wrapped this plant in plastic. I treat it like a work of art and place it on a pedestal where it belongs.

STYLING TIP Needing lots of warm, humid air, I'd style this plant in a sunroom, bathroom, or kitchen. Place it in a designer glazed planter to help keep the soil moist.

LIGHT The *Anthurium regale* is a shade and dappled light lover. Stay away from direct sun as this can burn the delicate foliage and kill the plant over time.

WATER Keep the soil moist but not wet. Take your finger and stick it about an inch/2.5cm down into the soil. If it's dry, its time to water the Regale. They thrive in humid climates in the wild, so placing them next to a humidifier and misting them once a week would be beneficial.

SOIL Make sure the roots are wrapped in a soil medium that is well aerated with a mix of bark, sphagnum moss, and organic potting soil. This will help keep the soil moist for longer and help your plant thrive.

TEMPERATURE Keep in an area of your home that stays between 65–75°F/18–24°C.

7 CODIAEUM VARIEGATUM 'GOLD DUST'

The 1990s called, they want their acid-washed plant back. Well guess what—they can't have it. If you haven't noticed that the '90s are back, from fashion to design, you must be living under a rock. We have stepped into the DeLorean and are once again wearing acid-washed jeans, relaxing on acid-washed couches, and styling our acid-washed plants. This plant I speak of is the gold dust croton, *Codiaeum variegatum* 'Gold Dust'.

I LIKE TO CONSIDER HOW THAT PAINT-SPLATTERED/ ACID-WASHED LOOK WILL VIBE WITH THE ART OR PATTERNS THAT EXIST AROUND IT IN THE ROOM.

While it may look is if it's been sprinkled by a gold dust fairy, I've always thought of the gold dust croton as the Jackson Pollock plant because of its paint-splattered look, as if it just happened to be a plant that sat too close to one of his canvases and got caught in the dance of his paint application.

This sort of style has been around for a while now and has made its way into various art forms. From fine art to fashion or product design, the energy and uniqueness of splattered paint has always been intriguing. I recall how cool it was as a younger artist to walk around school with your paint-splattered clothes, looking as if you pulled an all-nighter painting. It was like wearing a badge that said "artist."

While some plants have only their shape to make them stand out from the rest, this croton really sets itself apart, becoming a living work of art through its foliage characteristics. So when styling it in a space, I like to consider how that paint-splattered/acid-washed look will vibe with the art or patterns that exist around it. The best way to help it stand out is to place it against a plain background, such as a white wall, so that it appears as a burst of color like paint on a white canvas. You can also place it in a simple pot so as not to draw attention away from the plant. While it can be a difficult one to care for indoors, it's an extraordinary work of art to add to any collection.

STYLING TIP A terra-cotta or clay planter will help the foliage stand out.

LIGHT Style this plant in any place that gets direct sun or bright indirect light. More sun is better for healthy growth.

WATER Give your croton a drink once the top 2in/5cm of soil dries out. If the plant is very thirsty, you'll see its leaves faint. In that case, immediately water until water comes out of the drainage hole and into the base tray.

SOIL Wrap the roots in a soil medium that is well aerated with a mix of bark, sphagnum moss, a bit of perlite, and organic potting soil. This will keep the soil moist for longer and help your plant to thrive.

TEMPERATURE Style this plant in areas of your home that stay at 60–75°F/16–24°C, avoiding direct drafts from air conditioners and heaters.

8 NEOREGELIA 'HANNIBAL LECTER'

Perhaps you're starting to pick up what I've been putting down. When designing a home with plants, you can dig deeper into your creativity by building a bridge between a plant and a piece of furniture, to complement or contrast with its look and feel. Finding a connection can be challenging, but designer plants make it much easier. For instance, one of the most timeless fashion and designer trends out there is animal print. From zebra-print jackets to cheetah-print rugs, getting "wild at home" (see what I did there?) has been in fashion since the days when primitive man had to wear animal hides for warmth. Being covered from head to toe in elk, bear, or even cheetah wasn't out of the ordinary. As we became more civilized, the hides were also worn to make a statement about our status in life.

So, if you're designing a room and you're looking for a touch of greenery to work with your faux-alligator ottoman, maybe bring in a crocodile fern (*Microsorum musifolium* 'Crocodyllus'). Or if you're looking to connect a plant with your faux-cowhide rug, look no further than the polka dot begonia (*Begonia maculata*). Lately in interior design, there has been a major uptick in the tiger trend. From tiger prints to images of tigers, you can find them everywhere, including throw pillows, rugs, wallpaper and curtains. If you're styling something wild with tigers, one of my favorite designer plants to bring in is the *Neoregelia* 'Hannibal Lecter'.

I know—the first time I heard the name of this bromeliad, I laughed out loud, too. That reaction came immediately after I cried out loud, because I had touched the jagged side of a leaf and drawn blood. It's a perfectly named plant. The saw-like edges of its foliage ask that you handle it at your own risk, but its tiger-like patterned foliage demands that you style it where it can be seen and admired. Treat it as if you're looking at art in a museum, and remember what my mother would always say to me: "See with your eyes, not with your hands."

When designing with animal prints in the home, you're looking to make a bold statement. That should be the same with the plants you're working into the space as well. While designer plants have a connection with some of the design trends out there, it's not always necessary to correlate them one to one. Just because you have a tiger-print pillow, it doesn't mean you have to pair it with a similar-looking plant. You could juxtapose it with a different animal-patterned plant with greater impact, for a truly bold design statement.

ITS TIGER-LIKE PATTERNED FOLIAGE DEMANDS THAT YOU STYLE IT WHERE IT CAN BE SEEN AND ADMIRED.

STYLING TIP Placing your *Neoregelia* 'Hannibal Lecter' on a mounted board of cork high up on a wall or in a pot on a shelf would give you the ability to take in its beauty, but stay away from its sharp and dangerous foliage.

LIGHT Keep this plant in an indirect or dappled-light spot in your home. As with most indoor plants, your aim should be to replicate the natural habitat of the plant. *Neoregelia* is a bromeliad from the rainforests of South America, so keeping it out of direct sun is important.

WATER Keep the soil evenly moist, watering at least twice a week during spring and summer and making sure to keep a small amount of water in the center cup. Once the colder months arrive, water a bit less frequently.

SOIL If planting 'Hannibal Lecter' in a pot, a mix of organic potting soil, sphagnum moss, and perlite is great. If mounting this plant on the wall, wrap the roots in sphagnum.

TEMPERATURE Keep this plant in an area of your home that stays at 65–75°F/18–24°C.

9 CALADIUM PRAETERMISSUM 'HILO BEAUTY'

Sometimes it can be difficult to describe someone or something you're enamored by. There's this void that pops up in your brain, as if you've forgotten what words are or how to formulate them. Like now, when I stare at this blank screen (well, it was blank before I started writing these words) I'm asking myself, "How would I describe 'Hilo Beauty'?". I look at the plant deeply, analyzing it and trying to find the right word. It's right there on the tip of my tongue. But really, it's much simpler than I'm making it out to be. Everything is right there in its name—Beauty. There's no other way to describe it. 'Hilo Beauty' has a foliage that outdoors can resemble a camouflage print. Indoors, its pattern resembles that of terrazzo stone.

THE FOLIAGE OF A PLANT CAN INSPIRE THE WAY A SPACE IS STYLED THROUGH THE LENS OF PATTERN, COLOR, AND TEXTURE.

Terrazzo has been an ultra-popular design trend over the past 10 years. Although its growing popularity may be slowing down at this current moment, it still has a place in the hearts of designers, who have fashioned it into tables, tiles, countertops, and my favorite, planters. Going back to the 18th century, terrazzo has made its mark in the design world. Its sleek, modern look can easily level up any space. Design trends come and go, but the charm of a natural material is enduring and timeless.

What I love about terrazzo is the unpredictability of the placement of colors and shapes in its surface. That randomness makes each piece feel so unique. The same could and should be said about the foliage of *Caladium praetermissum* 'Hilo Beauty'. It reminds us that, like every living thing, we are each unique in our own way.

The 'Hilo Beauty' can not only complement a terrazzo piece in a room, it can also provide the look and feel of terrazzo even when the real thing is absent. I love the idea that the foliage of a plant can inspire the way a space is styled through the lens of pattern, color, and texture, and that is especially true in the case of this *Caladium*. Just as a designer looks at adding gold accents to a terrazzo backsplash, they should also think of complementary materials to surround their 'Hilo Beauty'. If terrazzo looks great next to red oak or ash, you can safely assume that this plant would as well. Terrazzo is like an only child; it's a natural material that, when it is placed next to other materials, wants all of the attention. Understand that the 'Hilo Beauty' has that same energy. It definitely puts the "ME" in "Love me."

STYLING TIP Do yourself a favor and place this plant in a gold or concrete planter and let it go to work. It'll sit perfectly on top of a terrazzo or wooden coffee table.

LIGHT Find a place that gets bright indirect to medium light. The brighter the light, the bigger the foliage will be, but avoid direct sun.

WATER Keep the soil evenly moist but not damp. The best thing would be to use your finger to test the moisture level of the soil. Once the top inch/ 2.5cm of soil feels dry, give it lukewarm water. Mist weekly.

SOIL Plant in a soil medium that is well aerated with a mix of bark, sphagnum moss, perlite, and organic potting soil. This will keep the soil moist for longer and help your plant thrive.

TEMPERATURE Style this plant in areas of your home that stay at 65–85°F/ 18–29°C during the day and no cooler than 60°F/16°C at night. It's best to keep it out of the direct blast of air conditioners and heaters.

10

PHILODENDRON MELANOCHRYSUM

When the curtains close, the show's over. The end. *Fin*, for all my French-speaking folks out there. And when those curtains close, they do so with such grace. The soft velvet fabric of both panels silently coming together initiates the loud applause from the crowd. The curtains play a huge role in theater, and they do the same in the theater of home design. Having curtains cascading down your walls and over your windows doesn't just provide privacy, it also adds texture and depth to your decor. Sometimes, when I'm designing an interior space, I'll drape curtains along a wall that doesn't even have a window, just because I enjoy the soft look. Having curtains hang in a home is definitely on everyone's interior design bingo card.

Just like the coffee table, lamp, and couch, curtains are an interior-design staple. The curvature created as a curtain panel folds along a rod has the look of fluted columns and the feel of rolls on the back of a chinchilla. If those curtains are made out of velvet, then I could say they have a look and feel similar to that of the *Philodendron melanochrysum*.

This is not only one of my top 10 designer plants, it's also on my list of favorite plants I've ever had the pleasure of caring for. The soft and velvety green foliage dangling from its thin vines really does resemble velvet curtains hanging on a rod. When light hits each leaf at a certain angle, it's as though the curtains have opened and the show has started. However, this is one of those "look but don't touch" plants. Its delicate foliage definitely feels like velvet, but you'll just have to imagine that as too much touching of the leaves can damage the tissue of the plant over time.

I like to style *P. melanochrysum* where it can be seen and admired. If a room has velvet curtains or throw pillows, that's a great place for this plant. If the throw pillows are on the couch, style this philodendron on the coffee table. If you have velvet curtains, place the plant on the console table across the room. What you're looking for is balance. In some cases you just have to let this plant guide your hand and show you where it fits best.

STYLING TIP With the *Philodendron melanochrysum* being a vine plant with soft leaves, I suggest styling it in a terra-cotta or concrete planter to juxtapose the two textures. If you place a trellis or wooden pole inside the pot, this will encourage the vines to grow upward.

LIGHT Place in a spot that gets bright indirect light in order to see larger growth and more vibrant foliage. Dappled sunlight is great, but keep it away from direct sun from south- and west-facing windows because this can burn the leaves and kill your plant over time.

WATER When the top half of the soil is dry, water your *P. melanochrysum* with lukewarm water until runoff comes out of the drainage holes of the pot. When styling tropical plants, it's important to mimic their natural climate when possible, so adding humidity via a humidifier and misting weekly will be important.

SOIL Surround the roots with a mix that is well aerated and retains moisture. A mix of organic potting soil, sphagnum moss, and perlite is great.

TEMPERATURE Keep in an area that stays at 60–75°F/16–24°C.

WHEN LIGHT HITS EACH LEAF AT A CERTAIN ANGLE, IT'S AS THOUGH THE CURTAINS HAVE OPENED UP AND THE SHOW HAS STARTED.

STYLED SPACES
A PORTFOLIO OF FLORA

Whenever I'm asked what my title is, I say I'm a plant and interior stylist, an artist, and an author. If it didn't take so long to mention those three, I'd throw a few more titles in there. While you may be familiar with the first and last, not many are aware of my background as an artist. Yet it is this role that has made me the stylist, designer, photographer, filmmaker, and author that I am today.

I recall knowing at the age of five that I wanted to be an artist. While I wasn't sure exactly what kind of artist, I was pulled towards creativity. I would spend hours thinking up characters to sketch on the three-holed lined paper my older cousins used at school and was embarrassingly excited when I went from a pack of 8 Crayola crayons to the 64-color box. I was fascinated by the slight shift in each color and how they related to one another. This was just the first of many "life-changing" moments. I recall discovering the "rule of thirds" when it came to creating visual images and how, armed with this knowledge, creating impactful compositions was everything to me. Understanding how a color or item sits in relation to others became my new language. The day I saw the way the light danced in the paintings of Caravaggio or Sargent shook me. Those nuances affected me deeply, changing the way I viewed and created art. And I held onto them, utilizing those ideas in every piece I created. At some point, my path to becoming a painter took a side turn into the field of filmmaking. That in turn became a path into interior design. And the path led to a clearing, one that is surrounded by greenery, as I work as a plant stylist. The ideas I learned through my many years of art education are the same ideas that I utilize as a plant stylist.

Whether it is sweeping a paintbrush across a canvas or moving furniture from one position to another, seeing the results come together in a beautiful way has always inspired me to go further. Working as a plant stylist has pushed me to expand my knowledge of plants beyond their care to a deep understanding of the patterns, shapes, colors, and textures available. I feel very fortunate to have a job that allows me to utilize my creativity in a way that not only brings plants into someone's home but also helps to cultivate happiness for those who live alongside them.

As I've always said, it only takes one plant to change the atmosphere in a room. Some clients want me to create an entire jungle in their homes, others just ask for a few plants sprinkled here or there, while a few need guidance on styling plants they already possess. Whatever the ask may be, I find so much happiness in being a part of their journey in greenery. Join me as I walk you through eight beautiful spaces that I've styled with plants. I provide insights on where I find my inspiration, explain how I go about working with a client, and reveal how to make a space come to life. This is my portfolio of flora.

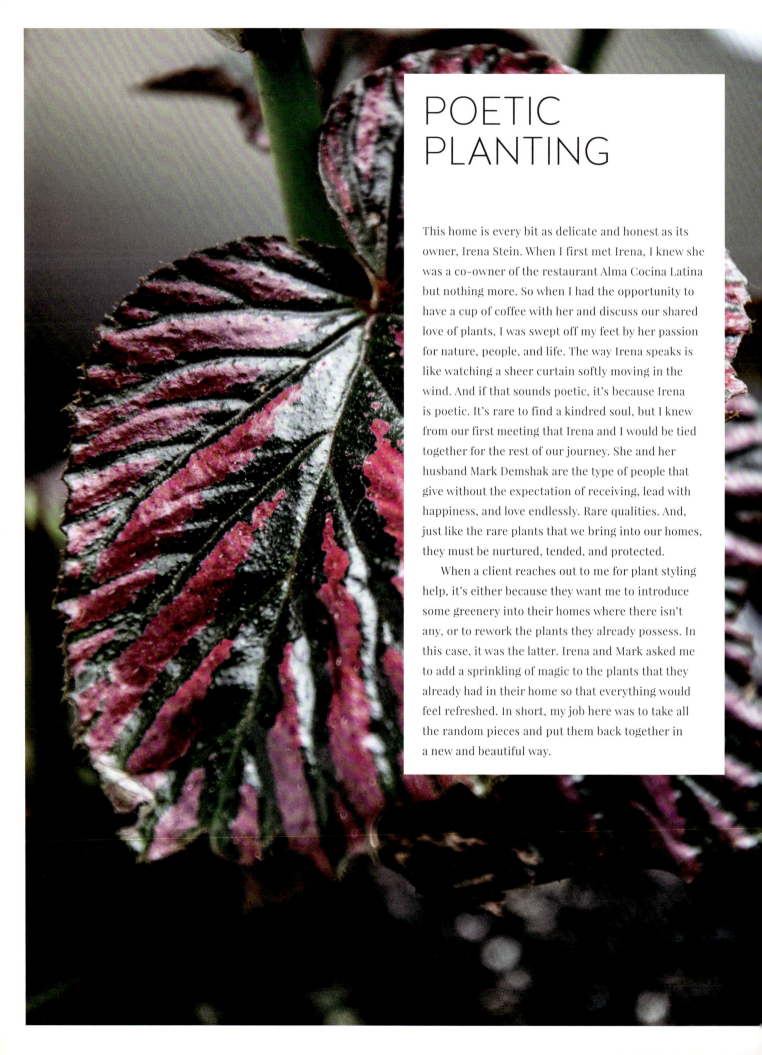

POETIC PLANTING

This home is every bit as delicate and honest as its owner, Irena Stein. When I first met Irena, I knew she was a co-owner of the restaurant Alma Cocina Latina but nothing more. So when I had the opportunity to have a cup of coffee with her and discuss our shared love of plants, I was swept off my feet by her passion for nature, people, and life. The way Irena speaks is like watching a sheer curtain softly moving in the wind. And if that sounds poetic, it's because Irena is poetic. It's rare to find a kindred soul, but I knew from our first meeting that Irena and I would be tied together for the rest of our journey. She and her husband Mark Demshak are the type of people that give without the expectation of receiving, lead with happiness, and love endlessly. Rare qualities. And, just like the rare plants that we bring into our homes, they must be nurtured, tended, and protected.

When a client reaches out to me for plant styling help, it's either because they want me to introduce some greenery into their homes where there isn't any, or to rework the plants they already possess. In this case, it was the latter. Irena and Mark asked me to add a sprinkling of magic to the plants that they already had in their home so that everything would feel refreshed. In short, my job here was to take all the random pieces and put them back together in a new and beautiful way.

As a child of Venezuela, lush environments are familiar to Irena. The idea of moving through densely planted environments and brushing past foliage to reach a destination is what she and I would call "a good problem to have." And in a home where there isn't much room to spread out, you're more than likely going to find a leaf or two caressing your hand as you move from one room to the next.

When a couple loves to host, their dining room must feel welcoming. Irena and Mark's vintage wooden dining table and chairs sit below the soft glow of a mid-century modern white globe pendant in the middle of the room. Around the perimeter, they originally had some dracaenas, evergreens, a snake plant (*Sansevieria trifasciata* var. *laurentii*), and a few others. My first step was to make sure these plants found themselves in the right spots, so that they could be enjoyed and well cared for. I started by shifting Irena's statement plant, a tall braided *Dracaena fragrans* (Deremensis Group) 'Lemon Lime' tree, from the center of a window to the corner of the room. Although it was enjoying a great light source by the window, the plant was blocking the path around the table and clogging the flow. Knowing it can tolerate medium light and that the corner sits between two large windows, I was confident that the dracaena would transition well there. I then moved the snake plant to sit beside the dracaena, given their similar foliage.

Looking at this room, you might think that either Irena chose the color palette of her plants based on the color palette of her chairs, or vice versa. Either way, I'm loving this look. To throw my hand into the mix, I found a large piece of wood on the couple's side porch and utilized it as a pedestal. Irena mentioned that this wood came from an old train yard, where it served as a post. One person's train yard post is another person's...ah, you get it! What grabbed my attention was its rounded edges and the warm yellow glow of the wood, which I thought would blend well with the yellows in the foliage of the plants beside it.

Now I needed the right plant to sit on top of the pedestal—something that was a work of art in its own right but could also tie the corner together. It had to be small enough to fit between the pompom of the 'Lemon Lime' dracaena and the spiny tips of the snake plant. Looking around the house, I found exactly the right addition—a *Ctenanthe oppenheimiana* 'Amagris' prayer plant. A member of the calathea family, easily recognizable by its violet underbelly, I knew the ctenanthe's frosty green topside, small stature, and striped pot would harmoniously bring the three plants together.

Playing with symmetry on a smaller scale, I grouped three plants on top of the vintage buffet, working them in among Irena and Mark's beautiful collection of pottery. To protect the buffet from moisture damage, I put felt pads under the base trays of the plants. To finish off the dining room, in the far corner and out of the way of heavy

IRENA AND MARK'S PASSION FOR LIFE IS INFECTIOUS AND THEIR DESIRE TO CULTIVATE LOVE AND HAPPINESS CAN SEEN THROUGHOUT THEIR HOME.

traffic, I placed a medium-size *Aglaonema* 'Silver Bay'. This lush beauty has an ability to tolerate lower light levels, so the distance from the window won't be an issue.

In the bedroom, the greenery is deliberately minimal to match the decor. Everything here feels thoughtfully placed and delicate. The color scheme projects a sense of calm, and when styling a bedroom your goal should always be to create that sort of feeling. A select few plants have migrated up from the ground floor, but only one makes a statement: in the far corner of the bedroom, a large *Philodendron selloum* sits on top of a wooden pedestal, its leaves reaching deep into the room. I merely tucked it closer into the corner and raised a few of the stems to grow upward instead of hanging outside the pot. Positioned between two windows facing north and west, the light level here is more than adequate. Meanwhile, on both nightstands small plants add a touch of life.

PLANTS ON PARADE
On top of a low sideboard in the living room, I styled a *Stromanthe sanguinea* 'Triostar', *Begonia brevirimosa*, and *Begonia* 'Lucerna' from Irena's plant collection. This simple and serene corner is a place where Irena's love for art, books and plants all comes together.

LUXURIANT LAYERS
Mark and Irena's spacious dining room is perfect for hosting both guests and plants. Utilizing the corners of the room when styling plants prevents them from getting in the way and makes it easier for people to move throughout the space while creating a great balance of greenery on both sides. I layered the heights of the plants in the right-hand corner to create an effect that mimics the way plants grow in nature.

SHADES OF GREEN

A grouping of clay vessels on the vintage buffet in the dining room holds a large variegated *Alocasia cucullata* and a small *Peperomia caperata* (left). Also known as Buddha's hand, the *Alocasia* has beautiful glossy variegated leaves (above). In the living room, Irena and Mark's collection of baskets and planters offers an intriguing variety of textures and forms, as do the plants. A philodendron with heart-shaped leaves cascades down one side of the bookcase with a flowering begonia on the other (opposite).

The side porch was where I got to truly show off my talents, taking a space that was being used to store unused planters and outdoor furniture and transforming it into an outdoor space for entertaining. Thanks to Irena's love of greenery, again I was working with plants that the couple already owned. In this case I worked in a large bamboo palm (*Chamaedorea seifrizii*) as the focal plant. Palms are one of my favorites because they instantly suggest a tropical vibe, and if the light is hitting right and a breeze is moving through, they will produce some of the most exquisite displays of dappled light you'll ever see.

To the right of the bamboo palm, I grouped together Irena's dieffenbachia, a *Phlebodium aureum* 'Blue Star' and a banana croton (*Codiaeum variegatum* 'Banana) to create a cluster of greenery. I played around with the plants to form a tiered effect, so they can all be seen and also to ensure that each one is easily accessible for proper care. On the far side of the porch, I pushed an outdoor coffee table that

wasn't being used into the corner and on top placed one of the couple's large *Aglaonema* 'Silver Bay' plants. Let me just say this, these two have a real love for Silver Bays. In this corner I let the Silver Bay stand alone to have its own moment and to balance the bamboo palm sitting catty-corner. For the finishing touches, I placed a small Rex begonia 'Escargot' and, from Irena's kitchen, a pot of Peruvian mint. Irena loves to entertain and feed her guests, so she dressed the table and topped it with a tart made with wild raspberries that she had picked from the side of the road the day before.

Irena and Mark's passion for life is infectious and their desire to cultivate love and happiness can be seen throughout their home and, on a larger scale, in their restaurant, Alma Cocina Latina (see pages 152–161). Luckily for me, I got the opportunity to help them style it.

A LEAFY ENCLAVE

The side porch is set up for an intimate brunch with friends. Setting the tone of this indoor/outdoor space is a huge bamboo palm (*Chamaedorea seifrizii*), which I chose to bring a breath of the tropics to this little slice of Baltimore, Maryland (opposite). In the other corner, an *Aglaonema* 'Silver Bay' sits in a concrete pot placed on top of a metal table to give it some added height and balance out the form of the bamboo palm (above). In another corner, a large and leafy *Philodendron* 'Green Congo' sits in a clay pot below a *Hoya carnosa* (left).

POETIC PLANTING

LUSH DETAILS

A sprawling *Philodendron selloum* on a low wooden stand makes a bold statement in the main bedroom. What I love about this philodendron is that its finger-like foliage looks as if it's reaching right into the center of the room (opposite). The nightstand is styled with a black-and-white portrait of a young Irena, piles of books and two small plants: *Peperomia caperata* and *Ctenanthe oppenheimiana* 'Amagris' (below). On the staircase, an *Aglaonema* 'Silver Bay' adds a splash of life and color. In the bathroom, a small potted *Peperomia tetragona* is slowly creeping its way along the vanity (below right).

POETIC PLANTING 119

ARTIST'S STATEMENT

How does one go about plant styling the home of an artist that they respect and admire? Well, plants are my medium and the home of Amy Sherald and Kevin Pemberton was my blank canvas. For Amy, paint is her medium and the blank canvas is, well... her canvas. Known as one of the greatest painters of our generation, Amy has a keen eye for color, form, and composition. So when she reached out to me and expressed her desire to have her new condo feel lush with an abundant of plants, I was floored.

I've known Amy for over 15 years now and consider her a friend, but she's like a big, big deal. A big-deal big deal. If I was going to style her home with plants, I needed to tap into my artist brain. Amy wanted lush, so I was going to bring luuuuuuush! But there was one issue. Amy's partner Kevin had his own idea of lush. You see, Kevin is an analytical thinker. Not someone who seeks chaos in his home. If Amy could be described as a wild, curved line, Kevin is a clean, straight one and stylish rather than thrifty, but I was ready to prove him wrong.

While Amy and Kevin's condo has an open-plan living space, the furniture has been arranged to create different zones for different activities, and I needed to find a theme to tie each area together. Drawing inspiration from the only hanging artwork in the room, the painting above the dining table, I decided to run with a desert theme. You don't see it? Really? In this abstract piece, I saw a mountain range in the Arizona desert at dusk. Now you see it! By artist Melissa Dickenson, the work is entitled "Lake Pagosa," and its tones of burnt sienna, sand, mustard, pinot noir, and creamy white would guide my hand when it came to choosing the plants and pots for this home.

It's a huge help here that the main source of light is a large, northeastern-facing wall of windows overlooking a shared courtyard. When styling the home of a plant novice, it also helps to choose plants that are on the low-maintenance side. With the light quality taken care of, my challenge was to find plants and planters that were just right for Amy and Kevin's aesthetic, but wouldn't detract from their great view.

With that at the forefront of my mind, I decided the sitting area was the place to make a statement. With its two tweed accent chairs and small wooden side table, this was somewhere I envisioned Amy and Kevin taking a moment in the day for themselves; to have a cup of coffee, sketch out ideas for a new project, or just reflect on life. To give this area that cozy appeal, a large plant was the way to start. I went with a 9-ft/2.7-m tall *Dracaena marginata*, because I wanted it to fill the space around and above the chairs. The condo ceiling is also 9ft/2.7m high, so the marginata just touches it. What I love most about this plant is the way its growth resembles fireworks. The upright branches remind me of the trails of smoke that shoot up into the sky, while its elegant, long thin leaves are the explosion of light. Positioning the *marginata* behind the chairs creates the effect of a little canopy of fireworks. As the foliage is long and ribbon-like and the branches are slender, light filters through and keeps the outside courtyard in view. The planter design was selected to echo the white pillars that the plant sits between and the color was pulled from the painting.

On the side table I placed a small *Monstera adansonii* in a gray modern ceramic planter and on the floor, nestled up to the table, a *Philodendron* 'Birkin' in a small terra-cotta planter. I selected the Birkin because the patterning of its foliage worked so well with the design of the chairs beside it. The richly colored planter adds a pop of color that pulls the eye from the terra-cotta leather couch back to the sitting area, tying the two areas together.

Between the sitting area and dining room is a spot where Amy and Kevin's dogs like to bask in the sun. I kept this area free, but utilized plants to separate the sitting area from the dining room. The last plant in the sitting area, before moving into the dining room, is a medium-size cat palm (*Chamaedorea cataractarum*). This is such a versatile plant, due to its ability to tolerate low light situations while also thriving in brighter light. However, I didn't position it here based on its light requirements, but because the foliage speaks the same language as the *marginata* while making a fuller, more robust statement. To maintain a balance, the cat palm is 5ft/1.5m in height compared to the lofty *marginata*. The variation in heights pleases the eye, while sitting here you feel fully embraced by greenery. A "plant hug," if you will. And who out there can't use a nice hug from time to time?

I decided to dress the palm in a leather-wrapped basket to create a sense of connection between the leather couch, the wooden arms of the accent chairs, and the shelving. When a plant is styled in a basket, or any planter that isn't waterproof, it's a good idea to keep it in its nursery pot. Place a base tray at the bottom of the basket, then put the plant in its nursery pot on top of that. This way, you're able to water the plant without damaging the basket or the surface below.

FOCAL POINT
In Amy and Kevin's bright living room, I styled a 9-ft/2.7-m *Dracaena marginata* to anchor the space and create a focal point in the room. The ceiling-to-floor windows let in a great blend of direct sun and bright indirect light throughout the day, and the addition of stylish modern lighting and the accent chairs nestled nicely between the greenery makes this corner the ideal spot for a lush sitting nook.

WHEN A PLANT IS STYLED IN A BASKET, OR ANY PLANTER THAT ISN'T WATERPROOF, IT'S A GOOD IDEA TO KEEP IT IN ITS NURSERY POT.

COLOR STORY
When styling an open floor space like this with plants, it's important to make sure there is a balance in the heights, colors, and styles of plants throughout the room (above). I created a little moment in the center of the dining table to connect the color story (above right). With my inspiration pulled from colors in the painting by artist Melissa Dickenson, I decided my color story for this home would be an earthy mix of burnt sienna, sand, mustard, pinot noir, white, and gold (opposite).

Moving into the dining room means moving away from the windows, which is why there are fewer plants here. To give this room its own statement plant, I went with a 7-ft/2.1-m burgundy rubber tree, or *Ficus elastica* 'Burgundy'. Its sleek, greenish-burgundy leaves are bisected by a thin red line, making it the perfect punch of living color to complement the colors in the painting.

As I've mentioned before, plant styling is all about seeing the full picture and understanding how to work the colors, shapes, and textures of your plants into the other design elements in your home. The rubber tree is potted in a fluted concrete planter that mimics the color and design of the nearby dining table and stools. Beside it is a *Caladium* 'Frog in a Blender', and this is the standout plant in the mix. The bright Kermit-green foliage patterned with speckles of lighter green screams for attention, which is why it's placed close to the dining table—it's a conversation starter. 'Frog in the Blender' is a work of art in the home of the artist. The gleaming gold planter reinforces its status and harks back to the gold floor lamp in the sitting room, giving the two areas a visual connection. The dining table centerpiece is a young *Philodendron selloum* in a yellow ceramic planter.

FINE VINES
When working with shelving, it's always nice to mix in a few vine plants that can cascade down the shelves (this page). I styled a *Dracaena fragrans* (Deremensis Group) 'Warneckei', with broad strokes of muted green along its strap-shaped foliage, in a fluted white clay pot with a raw clay base (opposite).

BLACK AND WHITE
A snake plant (*Dracaena trifasciata*) is perfect for empty corners or high-traffic areas because its upright growth keeps the leaves out of harm's way (left). Weezie, one of Amy and Kevin's three pups, finds sleeping in a tent surrounded by plants to be the perfect staycation (below). In the bedroom, I love to use plants that help remove pollutants from the air, such as snake plants and peace lilies (opposite).

Knowing that this table is often in use, I picked out a plant that doesn't take up too much space, yet has a large presence.

In the living room, I was limited both in terms of space and light. On the side of the couch closest to the windows is a *Dracaena fragrans* (Deremensis Group) 'Warneckei' that is the same height as the arm of the couch. On the built-in shelving, I added a few small ceramic planters holding plants such as a *Monstera adansonii* and an *Epipremnum pinnatum* 'Cebu Blue' vine, knowing that over time they will gently cascade down the shelves. Again, I pulled the colors of the planters from the Melissa Dickenson painting in the dining room.

Lastly, in the couple's bedroom, I introduced a large snake plant (*Sansevieria trifasciata* var. *laurentii*) in a tall black planter. I picked a snake plant for two reasons. Firstly, they are known to convert carbon dioxide into oxygen and purify the air, making them perfect for a bedroom. And, secondly, because this room doesn't get a lot of bright light. Across the room, next to a peace lily (*Spathiphyllum*), which was the only plant Amy and Kevin already had that was loving life when I arrived, I placed a *Dracaena* Gold Star. With its upright form, I knew it would slot into the corner without taking up too much space.

I left Amy and Kevin's home feeling great about the plantings I'd created and the way it would leave them feeling too. Once I got a moment, I sent over notes on how to care for everything I had brought in. I added brushstroke after brushstroke to my artwork—now it just needs time to dry.

WOOD GRAINS AND CONCRETE PLAINS

Clavel is not just one of the best Mexican restaurants in Baltimore, Maryland, but one of the best in the United States. It is owned by Carlos Raba, Lane Harlan, and Matthew Pierce, whose collective vision was to bring the mood, textures, and colors of Sinaloa and Oaxaca, Mexico, to Baltimore.

As soon as you enter the building, Clavel absorbs your five senses and instantly transports you to Mexico. You can see it in the concrete walls, floors, and bar, the carefully selected wooden pieces that make up the stools and shelving, and the woven textures of the baskets and light pendants. It is evident in the flavors and smells of the food and drink, and the sounds of the music mingling with the sounds of those dining. No passports are necessary, but a trip to Mexico is what's on offer here. Even without the addition of plants, Clavel is lush and lovely. And all of this is what made me think it would be the perfect place for a first date. That first date took place at Clavel, and the individual I took on that date is now my wife. Needless to say, Clavel and its three owners have a very special place in both our hearts.

When I was given the opportunity to design the planting at Clavel, I wanted to stay true to the vision that Carlos, Lane, and Matthew started out with and still have today. To do so, I decided to bring in only plants that were either from Mexico or are commonly seen there. I also wanted to make sure that the pottery these plants would be dressed in was either Mexican or in harmony with the textures and colors of Mexican pottery. When it came to choosing the plants, the most obvious one was the blue agave plant, or *Agave tequilana*—it is used to create tequila, so utilizing that connection would have been a no-brainer. But when you're working on a high-traffic area, with large numbers of guests moving through the restaurant from the time the doors open until last call, agave plants might not be the best choice. Yes, they will transport you to Mexico by their look, but they may also transport you to the emergency room with their feel. Agave tends to grow outward, stretching its thorn-tipped foliage into the available surroundings, ready to poke the first bit of flesh that intrudes into its space. I get it—we all need our personal space—but to stab someone for it is a little, you know, excessive. But I digress.

When I think about which plants to bring into a space, I look for those that will make the biggest statement or impact. But, to be honest with you, here I wanted every plant to make a statement, and each and every one was carefully selected for exactly the right spot in the restaurant. The goal wasn't to make this an overly lush experience, but to keep it true to the look and feel of Mexico and to the aesthetic of the artists that created the space. When plant styling, my job is to play my instrument in tune with the other musicians in the orchestra. So if Lane is playing the guitar beautifully, I won't come in with a guitar and try to play it louder. Instead, I'll bring in a trumpet and fall into the folds of the guitar's notes so that the sounds are harmonious.

The *nixtamal* room was where most plant styling was required. This is the newest addition to the restaurant and, without a doubt, has the best natural light. It is where the *nixtamal* (limed kernels of corn) is turned into *masa* (maize dough) to make tortillas and chips for the restaurant. It's also a waiting area for patrons and showcases a few gift items. In short, this room is what I would describe as the "welcome" moment at Clavel. And what a beautiful welcome it is! Much of that beauty is down to its simplicity and minimalism, so I provided only what I felt would add to the moment, not take away from it.

At the end of one of the two narrow tables that protrude from the walls, I placed an aloe. As the tables are fairly short, I wanted to make sure the plants wouldn't take up too much space, so going with a slow-growing aloe (*Aloe vera*) was important. Aloe plants can be found throughout Mexico, but my main reason for using it here was its bold, sculptural form and the dash of green it adds to this area. I dressed it in a modern terra-cotta pot. In fact, you'll notice that almost all the plants I styled here are in terra-cotta pots, a choice based on their color and texture. The terra-cotta helps to highlight the warm tones you see dotted elsewhere and move the eye from one side of the room to the other.

> WHEN PLANT STYLING, MY JOB IS TO PLAY MY INSTRUMENT IN TUNE WITH THE OTHER MUSICIANS IN THE ORCHESTRA.

At the other end of the same table, I decided to position a plant on the step below, so I needed something with a trunk tall enough to lift its foliage above the table, well out of the way of those sitting under it. A large ponytail palm (*Beaucarnea recurvata*) fitted the bill perfectly. With this at one end and the aloe at the other, the seating area creates an inviting vignette.

Across the room, on the parallel wall, is an identical table. For the sake of keeping balance in the unbalanced, I styled this table with a single, intriguing plant—a Madagascar palm (*Pachypodium lamerei*). While this palm has large thorns that can harm you if you're not careful, introducing a small one in a quieter area is fine. Vistors to a museum understand that they can walk around a work of art and take in all its beauty, but it's a "look but don't touch" situation. The same goes for this palm. Enjoy it—but keep your hands to yourself.

VINE DINING
An imposing *Monstera adansonii* totem in an urn-shaped clay planter stands beside the kitchen door. With a vine plant like this one, you can train the vines to climb the wall using hooks or small staples until the nodes of the vines grab onto the wall and fully become a part of the space.

At the back of the room, I felt there was a need for a bigger presence—one that would catch the eye upon entering. I decided a large *Monstera adansonii* totem would be the best way to give this area a punch of life. Set against the wall between the back doors and the counter, it's a striking presence. Over time, the vines will grow up and along the wall, becoming one with the space. This monstera is the only plant that isn't placed in a terracotta pot. Here, I went with a planter that almost blends into the concrete wall, allowing for the transference of plant to wall to seamlessly take shape.

In front of the monstera sits a peace lily (*Spathiphyllum wallisii*) that was already in the store. When a client owns plants that they want to retain, I find an opportunity to give that plant a new position. On the side wall across from the peace lily, a wooden shelving unit holds wine and other items for sale. I dressed this with two plants. Yes, the same type of plant, but two different varieties. On the top shelf I placed a small variegated prickly pear (*Opuntia*), while on the floor, to the left of the shelf, I went with a larger, regular prickly pear. These are typically slow-growing and almost thornless, making them safe in restaurants or other busy areas.

QUIET MOMENTS

One of my favorite things about Clavel, beyond the amazing cuisine, is the mix of natural textures and tones. Woven pendant lighting hangs above the concrete counter (opposite above left). A *Rhaphidophora tetrasperma* clambers up the wall (opposite above right) while a Madagascar palm perches at the edge of a shelf (opposite below right). A lofty *Euphorbia trigona* stands tall in the quiet entry (opposite below left). A detail of the intricate *Rhaphidophora tetrasperma* foliage (this page).

One of the best sources of light in any space is a skylight. And as one of the Clavel dining rooms has not one, not two, but three skylights positioned at equal intervals in the room, a few decisions were made for me when it came to choosing plants. I wanted the statement plant here to be a force—something structural, abstract in its growth, and raw. A plant with a real presence, which you could see possibly growing out of the building one day.

Having considered a few different options, I kept coming back to a yucca plant, knowing that its size and the wild energy of the plant would provide the desired "wow" moment. Yuccas are known for being low maintenance when it comes to moisture, but high maintenance when it comes to light. At Clavel, the large skylight directly above not only provides the perfect source of illumination for this yucca to thrive, but also means that its growth is directed upward. Plants will always grow in the direction of a light source, so if the source is above, that's where this beauty will stretch its branches. And in a high-traffic space like a restaurant, having plants that don't grow outward is beneficial. To dress the yucca, I placed it in a traditional terra-cotta pot that plays off the rich tones in the brick walls and the warmth of the wooden tables.

Below another skylight and above the Mezcal bar, I hung a large fishbone cactus (*Disocactus anguliger*) in a terra-cotta planter, allowing its serrated, zigzagging foliage to tumble downward. Ok, it might be a little obvious, but yes—I went with the fishbone cactus here to play off the fact that they serve fish tacos at Clavel and I, for one, love everything about a fish taco.

THE DESERT'S IN THE DETAILS
These shelves hold items for sale that allow guests to take a little touch of Mexico home with them, next to two prickly pear cacti (*Opuntia*) that sit on top of and beside the shelving (above left). The prickly pear cactus is a Mexican staple, with blooms that are produced during spring and summer (above right). A large yucca makes the perfect statement as guests enter the second dining room (opposite).

FISHBONES AND MEZCAL
A large fishbone cactus (*Disocactus anguliger*) hangs above the Mezcal bar because it has the perfect shape and the perfect name. While the fish tacos here are served boneless, the connection felt right. I placed a large yucca to the side of the staircase to bring warmth and color to an empty corner (opposite).

A ROOM WITH A VIEW

What is a loggia, you ask? Well, I asked myself that same question. Honestly, I'm still not sure if I know exactly, but the outdoor space where Megan Isennock and Rob Tate entertain, eat family dinners with the kids, and find an escape from the inside of their home, which is only 37 Hilton-sized-shoes wide (yes, I measured it, and I wear a size 15 shoe), was described to me as such. The all-knowing *Webster's Dictionary* describes it as "a roofed open gallery, especially at an upper story overlooking an open court." While I'm still uncertain whether this beautiful space is indeed a loggia, I'm certain that I like saying the word "loggia." It sounds so fancy rolling off my tongue. Say it with me… "loggia." See, fancy! But if you're uncomfortable rolling your "g's," in layman's terms you can call it an outdoor sunroom. Believe me, there is no shame in that. What is a sunroom, you ask? Seriously?! If you don't know what a sunroom is by now, we're going to have a hard time trying to connect. The qualification of any sunroom is that there must be light. And this one has plenty of that. The qualification for an amazing sunroom is that there must be plants basking in said sun. And it's this last ingredient that was lacking in Megan and Rob's sunroom, which is where someone like myself makes their grand appearance.

Whenever I find myself in a situation where there is an abundance of light, I'm like a kid in a candy store. In terms of plant styling, all options are now on the table. Especially when the main source of light is a large skylight that sits above the center of the room like a halo above an angel or—and hear me out here—like an actual greenhouse. I mean let's be honest, this sunroom is basically a greenhouse that isn't climate controlled. When it comes to plant care, the right light is the most important thing you can give a plant, and if you're able to provide it from a source above, you'll see your plants absolutely thrive. So while I had enough room to go completely wild in this sunroom and drape plants from every angle, the goal was to make sure the space still felt open, airy, and bright. You can see that without plants —without that pop of green, that touch of life—this space could look and feel chilly and drab. And while the colder months play a large role in this, it's the coming together of indoor and outdoor elements, come spring, that really bring the sunroom to a rejuvenated state.

What I love about Megan and Rob's sunroom is the way it takes on the identity of an outdoor living/dining room, all the while nestled up to a small swimming pool. The couple's Federal-style home in Baltimore City was built in 1854, but this type of charm is fresh, with the pool and sunroom added in 1999. It was the beauty of the wisteria vines caressing the brick wall separating the pool and sunroom that provided me with the inspiration I needed.

Once I entered the sunroom, the second thing that grabbed my attention (the first being the light source above and the bright white floor and ceiling) was the built-in planter boxes that formed part of the built-in seating. When I chatted with Megan about this area of the room, she mentioned that she could never figure out what to plant in the boxes due to the changing seasons and also because her cats treated these planters like their personal litter boxes and loved to dig out the soil. I'm sure many of you can relate. With these obstacles in mind, my initial move was to figure what the plan should be regarding adding greenery.

With the fall and winter climate in Baltimore, Maryland, dropping way below the temperature necessary for tropical plants to live, and the fact that this sunroom is utilized mostly from the spring through early fall, I thought it best to create a tropical space for that timeframe, with the plan being that all the plants would be moved indoors once the colder months arrived. With that in mind, I took a walk around the interior of the home, working out where the outdoor plants will live once they come inside in the fall. This meant that all the plants in the planter boxes would remain in their nursery pots to make the transitions much easier.

As I mentioned earlier, plant styling any space starts with creating a theme. For Megan and Rob's sunroom, that theme was "garden party." Once I had that in mind, the next step was choosing the right plants. For the built-in planter boxes, I needed plants that were hardy and could stand up to high-traffic areas and being moved in and out. I also had to be mindful of the quality of light in this area of the room. Using a light meter is the most accurate way of determining light quality, but over time I've learned how to eyeball it, or to just count the distance in feet from the plant to the light source. Here, for best results, I needed to use plants that could tolerate medium to low light levels. My selection included *Monstera deliciosa*, yucca plants, *Philodendron* 'Rojo Congo' and 'Green Emerald', and cat palms (*Chamaedorea cataractarum*). I filled the planters with soil, which lifted the plants higher in the boxes. After that, I placed the plants in their desired spots. I liked the idea of the planters being bookended with palms, to add height, then gradually stepping down the size of the plants toward the center of the box. Once I was happy with the positioning, I added the remaining soil, making sure that the plastic pots were covered.

PATIO POTTED
I styled a single large majestic palm (*Ravenea rivularis*) in terra-cotta to brighten up this nook without crowding it (opposite above left). The built-in wooden planters hold tropical plants that can grow larger over time. A yucca plant and a cat palm (*Chamaedorea cataractarum*) add life and warmth to the aged bare brick walls. The white stones look clean and keep the couple's pet cats away from the plants (opposite above and below right). *Codiaeum variegatum var. pictum* 'Petra' is an eyecatching centerpiece on the low coffee table (opposite below left).

SMALL BITES
Megan's bar cart is ready and waiting for a party, dressed with beverages and plant life (top). Asparagus ferns hang down from the ceiling, pushing their fronds up and out toward the bright light from the skylight (top right). The dining table is dressed for a garden party by stylist Adel Ainslie, with floating floral petals in shallow dishes and small plants dotted along the table (above).

Now I just had one last obstacle to address…the cats. Oh, the feline community. For many of us plant parents, it's a delicate balance between loving our plants and loving our cats. To help discourage Megan and Rob's cats from using the planter boxes as litter boxes, I carefully covered the topsoil with a layer of small stones. This not only solved the cat problem, given that our feline friends despise walking on sharp, pebbly surfaces, but also helped to make the boxes look crisp and presentable. This is important given that guests enjoying these areas will most likely be sitting at eye level with the base of the plants.

My next goal was to address the skylight. As I explained in my first book, *Wild at Home*, my go-to when styling a space is to use lots of different levels. This mimics the way that plants grow in nature, placing them at ground level, eye level, and higher. For this area of the room, I wanted to add hanging plants that would cascade down and grow outward as well. I selected four large black metal hanging baskets with coconut liners—the typical hanging baskets that you find in an outdoor garden. But when it came to the plant selection, I decided to be a little atypical. In most situations like this, give a designer a hanging basket and they'll place a Boston fern (*Nephrolepis exaltata*) in there without giving it a second thought. While I love that look, I wanted a plant that felt airy and is seldomly utilized—the asparagus fern (*Asparagus setaceus*). Once they were potted and hung around the center of the room, these ferns really started to give the sunroom life.

MY GO-TO WHEN STYLING A SPACE IS TO USE LOTS OF DIFFERENT LEVELS. THIS MIMICS THE WAY THAT PLANTS GROW IN NATURE.

WARM MOMENTS
The wood-burning stove sits patiently awaiting a cold night, when it will keep Megan and her family and friends warm. During the warmer seasons, firewood is stacked beside the stove. A safe distance away sits a macho fern (*Nephrolepis biserrata*) enjoying the bright indirect light that feeds the room.

PARTY VIBES
The outdoor sunroom is full of life, color, and light. It's a very versatile space as it is covered and has a wood-burning stove, so it can be used throughout the year for sociable get-togethers, parties, and other occasions. However, I can't say the same thing about the tropical plant life here—that needs to make its way indoors for the winter once the nighttime temperatures drop below 50°F/10°C.

WALL ART
A crocodile fern (*Microsorum musifolium* 'Crocodyllus') is mounted on cork next to an antique candelabra. Mounted plants add great depth to a room and the texture and shape of the fern's foliage play well against the brick (left). An empty white frame allows the brick wall to become the art (below left). In this corner of the sunroom, I created a small sitting area for guests. A huge *Ficus binnendijkii* 'Alii' makes a statement here—it fills the corner perfectly and sets a bold tropical vibe for the space (opposite).

I then started to create small pockets or "moments" that create a statement without overcrowding the room. Next to one of the built-in benches, I potted a large majestic palm (*Ravenea rivularis*). I love using these plants in indoor spaces because there's nothing that says "tropical" more than a palm. I chose to place it in a terra-cotta pot to play off the warm reds in the brick walls and the bright pops of color that Megan and Rob like to see in their pillow and dinnerware selections.

The next "moment" I wanted to address was the corner of the sunroom. As this part of the room has a lofty ceiling height of 9ft/2.7m, I had the opportunity to really allow a plant to shine. To achieve this, the best option is a tree. And to know me is to know I love a good ficus tree. Again wanting to create a light and airy effect, I went with a graceful *Ficus binnendijkii* 'Alii', popping it in a terra-cotta pot to tie the room together.

With most jobs, I find clients already own plants that they have begun caring for and given a nice spot in their home. In these situations, I take what's there and rework it to fit my theme. Moving Rob and Megan's macho fern (*Nephrolepis biserrata*) to an open area gives it new life, while clustering a few plants here and there again creates nice vignettes around the sunroom. The transformation of this space was a beautiful thing to see, and I hope Megan and Rob will enjoy it for many seasons to come.

POOLSIDE PLEASURES
The tranquil pool sits below a lush green wisteria vine. During the spring and summer months, both pool and wisteria are at their most desirable. Deck lounge chairs and a table are tucked nicely under a striped umbrella and against a canopy of wild grape vines (opposite). This is all part of Baltimore's leafy charm.

MIXED GREENS

Alma Cocina Latina restaurant in Baltimore is a love letter to Venezuela, or at least that's how it seems to me. When someone takes so much time and effort to articulate the beauty and soul of a place, to create a feeling or a mood that is so endearing, what else can one call it but a love letter? A homage, maybe? That's probably the right word, but for owners Irena Stein and Mark Demshak, I think I'll stick with love letter. You can see it in the details painstakingly woven into the fabric of the interior. From the flavors of the cuisine to the textures of the decor, from the painted murals to the warm smiles of the staff, from the music to the tempting smells from the kitchen—it's all a taste of what Irena calls home.

Irena, who spent her childhood in Caracas, has bottled up a taste of Venezuela and serves it to the people of Baltimore. It's her gift to the city. Once you pass through the doors of Alma, you are instantly transported to South America. Now that I think about it, maybe Alma Cocina Latina is not only a love letter to Venezuela, but also a love letter to Baltimore. When you've found a connection that is profound, you want to show and share as much of yourself as you possibly can. And this is exactly what Irena has done at Alma—thrown her arms open wide, ready to envelop the city in a warm embrace.

As with Irena and Mark's home (see pages 108–119), my job at the couple's restaurant was to help them rework their greenery in a more effective and impactful way. While there is no doubt that Alma is known for its food, it's just as well known for its atmosphere. And one of the biggest components of said atmosphere is the abundance of plant life here. Anyone who knows me will tell you that I'm on a constant search for the "wow." And in Alma, that's what I found.

While the plants that create the interior's "jungle-liciousness" may not be native to Venezuela, the way in which Irena and Mark have collected them, in a generous and open-hearted fashion, is typical not only of Venezuela but also of the plant-loving community I am myself deeply rooted in. You see, many of the plants at Alma were gifted to Irena and Mark, either as gestures of kindness or gratitude, or because the owner of the plant could no longer care for it in a way that would allow the plant to thrive. As a result, the restaurant is a bit of a plant rescue center. And a beautiful one at that. Many of the plants are mature and have grown broad and tall, long and wild. As a plant grows older, it begins to reveal its individuality and unique energy. It may have a few areas of leaf loss, or perhaps its branches have grown toward a light source, bending and curving into the shape it is today. Just like us, plants are works in progress, and I love that about them.

Even though many of the plants here were gifted, together they feel like they're all one big happy family. Just like any family, there's a quirky yet beautiful mix of characters. You can find Norfolk Island pines (*Araucaria heterophylla*), *Philodendron xanadu*, fiddle-leaf figs (*Ficus lyrata*), bamboo palms (*Chamaedorea seifrizii*), and many more scattered throughout the restaurant. Despite the wealth of large plants battling for star status, it was the weeping figs (*Ficus benjamina*) that I decided to take to the next level. In the center of the restaurant, a large open partition with two wide shelves separates the bar area from the main dining room. When thinking about how to create a better sense of flow and integration using the existing plants, it was this partition that dominated the space and presented my biggest challenge. Irena had styled a few plants in baskets on the top shelf, but other than that it was pretty bare. I knew the best place to start would be to put plants on and around the partition to make it feel cohesive.

STATEMENT MADE
Thanks to its custom-made pedestal, this outsize *Ficus benjamina* is now the first thing guests see as they enter the restaurant, setting the tone for what's to follow. The raw concrete pot was chosen as it pairs well with the textures of the metal beams and parquet flooring (opposite).

JUST LIKE US, PLANTS ARE WORKS IN PROGRESS, AND I LOVE THAT ABOUT THEM.

My initial thought was to bookend the partition with two large weeping figs. But instead of placing them on the floor, I wanted to raise them up so that when entering the dining room they were the first thing you would see. I knew that at that height they would sit above any foot traffic through the restaurant but I was concerned that there wasn't enough space on the shelf at either end of the partition to hold plants of such size. While planning how best to achieve this look, I suggested to Irena and Mark that placing them on pedestals could be a great solution. Wanting to keep the look of the pedestals consistent with the rest of the space, the couple had two custom-made from wood and metal. This gave the weeping figs and their gorgeous pots a new home where they now stand out from everything around them. On the top shelf, I placed a large *Philodendron xanadu* in the center of the grouping of baskets. This adds a splash of color and pulls the attention of the guests into both sides of the room, creating a tunnel of green through the dining room. With its lush growth spilling down over the shelf, this glorious philodendron is just begging for attention.

With so much greenery to work with, I needed to make sure that I gave the design structure. It's easy to accumulate a lot of plants in a desire to bring the outdoors in and then push them against the wall or as close to a window as possible. For me, there is artistry in deciding how to best situate plants in a room, so they can not only receive care from their owners but also show off their leafy and luscious good looks to best advantage.

SETTING THE VIBE
I used plant groupings to create intimate moments in the restaurant by separating one table from another and to make this high-ceilinged space feel more cozy (top). The blooms of a begonia add a vibrant pop of color (above). An intricate gilded mirror helps to reflect light around the room (above right). A view of the long and leafy plant-filled dining room at Alma (opposite).

While Alma may have a lot of windows, not a great deal of natural light makes its way deep into the building's interior. Accordingly, at the end of service every day, the majority of the plants here are wheeled close to the windows, then before the restaurant opens again they are pushed back and styled in the positions that you see in these photographs. The variable light levels is one reason why many of the plants are mounted on casters. The other reason is to ensure maximum flexibility and prevent Irena and Mark from being locked into one particular look. As the plants are mobile, it's easy to make quick changes and edits. If the lofty Norfolk Island pine doesn't sit right between two tables as initially thought, or is growing too large for the space, moving it to another area of the restaurant isn't a big deal in the same way it would be if it were potted in a heavy ceramic planter. While I'm not usually a fan of the look of casters under planters, in this situation it's a case of function over form and it works perfectly.

Knowing that it would be easy to swap different plants in and out as needed, I allowed the flow of the space to guide me, observing how guests interact with the room and trying not to impede on their experience but to gently submerge them in layers of greenery. One of the things that I felt would keep the allure intact was to move one of the mobile screens that separates one table from the main dining room to the other end of the space, where it conceals the swinging doors into the kitchen. While you might think I've stripped the privacy away from that particular table, my goal here was to bring it into the party and keep all the technical stuff "backstage."

THE DINING ROOM

Alma feels like a small part of Venezuela in Baltimore. The rooster and fish murals by Venezuelan artist Elisa Murillo loom large while lush layers of greenery welcome diners and draw them into the space. Invoking a warm and welcoming mood is what Mark and Irena have baked into Alma. The mix of plant life is down to the fact that Irena was given many of the plants here to care for because others could not. Her nurturing spirit is at the heart of this space.

ALL IN THE DETAIL
Irena arranges small bouquets along the bar to set the mood (above left). A small painting of caged macaw parrots by Venezuelan artist Pablo Antonio Millan hangs on a wall in the restaurant—just one of the many works of Venezuelan art showcased here (left). An imposing *Philodendron xanadu* is perched high above the dining room, providing a dramatic centerpiece. Below sits a money tree (*Pachira aquatica*) and an *Aglaonema* 'Silver Bay', creating a touch of privacy between the tables (above).

Irena and Mark presented me with a space that was already full of life and I made small adjustments to make it easier for the guests and staff to enjoy that space. I lifted plants higher in the room, creating generous canopies and conversation starters. I rotated taller plants, so that their foliage leans into the space and brings energy to the center of the room, and pushed smaller plants to the edges of tables to create balance. As a child, when I was given a box of crayons and sat down to draw, I always used every single color available. Here, I felt the same need to use every plant given to me and make it a part of the finished work of art. And Alma Cocina Latina is truly that—a work of art, brimming with color, texture, and detail. Irena and Mark may have created this pocket of Venezuela as a love letter to Baltimore, but I hope I was able to utilize their plants to articulate my love for them. XOXO

NEIGHBORS

In the home of Shawn and Anne Chopra, you'll find a beautiful mix of stylish Danish-designed furnishings, wood-paneled ceilings, a vintage record player, an impressive collection of art and design books, and a coffee machine that only an Italian barista would understand how to operate. What you won't find is a dark corner, and that's because most of the walls in this home are made out of glass.

For a residence with so many windows, I had a hard time understanding why there weren't more plants here. No judgment, but if you're given the gift of natural light, why would you not take full advantage and turn your home into an indoor jungle? To me, that's like living on a basketball court but not having any basketballs. But, all jokes aside, when my business partner Shawn, owner of *good neighbor*, a boutique coffee and furniture shop, and co-owner of *green neighbor*, the best plant shop in the world (yes, I'm biased, but whatever) approached me about helping him plant style his home, I was honored. This is a man with a great eye for design but a (self-described) brownish thumb when it comes to plants. Adding a touch of lushness to Shawn and Anne's home would be my pleasure.

When you're working with this amount of available light, your options for plants become pretty much endless. The only parameters are whatever works best with the design and decor of the home, and the care capabilities of the individuals looking after the plants. Shawn and Anne would be going from 0 to 60 in 2.6 seconds, so I needed to make sure I left them with all the necessary tips on how to maintain the plants with which I styled their home.

With three floors to work across, I decided to start on the first floor, where Shawn's office and lounge are located. On most jobs, I start with the types of plants that will work best in the space, then find the right planters, but here I thought it would be better to source planters that aligned well with the decor throughout. In the office, I went with modern planters that were sleek and simple and meshed with the color palette of the room.

On Shawn's desk I kept it scaled back, with a *Peperomia tetragona* taking up the smallest amount of real estate possible—Shawn's paperwork and other business materials occupy most of the space here, and I wanted to minimize the risk of exposing the electronics to moisture. I placed the peperomia in a light green planter to amplify the foliage of the plant and to provide a vibrant pop of color. Behind the desk, against the wall, I potted a medium-size ZZ plant, or *Zamioculcas zamiifolia*, in a sleek modern raw clay pot. As this corner is approximately 6ft/1.8m from the nearest window, it needed a plant that could tolerate low light and a certain lack of attention. I decided on the raw clay planter because its warm, earthy hue complements the wood chair beside it and the frame of the artwork above.

On Shawn's bookshelf, I added a few vine plants that cascade down gracefully, while just to the right, in a curvaceous black metal planter, I placed a *Dieffenbachia*

POPS OF GREEN
A variety of leaf shapes and colors enliven Shawn and Amy's home, including (clockwise from opposite, above left) a *Peperomia tetragona*; a leafy *Dieffenbachia*; a ZZ plant in a terra-cotta pot that harmonizes with the chair and artwork above it; and vine plants tumbling down Shawn's bookshelf.

hybrid. Again, as this spot is a little distant from the nearest window, choosing a plant that can tolerate this light quality is key. I love the *Dieffenbachia* foliage against the black leather Eames lounge chair and its similarity to the ink application on the artwork above it.

Make your way upstairs to the second floor, and you're in the area of the home that sees the most foot traffic—the kitchen, dining room, and living room. When plant styling any high-traffic areas, the goal is always to make sure you aren't creating trip hazards or clutter. There's no point placing a plant where it blocks an area of the home so those that live there have to move it back and forth to access that particular area.

As I explain in *Centerpieces* (see pages 38–41), the center of the dining or kitchen table is the perfect spot for a small, unique plant. Here, I went with an olive tree (*Olea europaea*) and dressed it in a white clay pedestal planter, styling the top of the soil with toning small white stones. I chose an olive because it's a perfect tie-in with food as well as a great indoor plant in a room with abundant

> WITH MOST JOBS, I START WITH THE TYPES OF PLANTS THAT WILL WORK BEST IN THE SPACE THEN FIND THE RIGHT PLANTERS.

direct sunlight. When working with small planters that will sit on a table where guests may be eating, I typically like to hide the soil with stones or moss. This gives it a clean, polished look and helps to deter pests.

Above the table, I hung a kangaroo fern (*Microsorum diversifolium*) and below it, in a small black metal planter, a *Philodendron selloum*. I wanted a statement piece for the top of the marble island, so went with a burgundy rubber tree (*Ficus elastica* 'Burgundy') in a white molten-effect metal planter. The dark leaves of the rubber tree protruding from the glossy white planter create a striking effect. On the counter, next to the coffee machine, I placed a small coffee plant (*Coffea arabica*) in a ribbed glazed planter. Yes, I went completely literal here—I placed a coffee plant next to a coffee machine. But wait, I'm not done. I also made sure the planter was cream colored. Oh yeah, watch me work! Lastly, to finish off the kitchen, I placed a large

ON THE BRIGHT SIDE

With floor-to-ceiling windows and a generous flow of natural light, Shawn and Anne's kitchen gave me many options for plant styling (left). A dainty olive tree (*Olea europaea*) brings life to the center of the kitchen table and I dressed the top of the soil with stones to keep the look clean (above). Why not have a coffee plant (*Coffea arabica*) to accompany the coffee machine? That's exactly what I went for here (below left). I placed a rubber tree (*Ficus elastica*) on top of the kitchen island to raise the viewpoint in the room higher (opposite).

lady palm (*Rhapis excelsa*) in a gray concrete planter. Some height was needed to balance the hanging fern and the rubber tree on the island and I love dropping in a lady palm whenever possible—they have such a lively presence and can tolerate many types of light situations.

In the dining room I kept it low-key. Letting the live-edge wood dining table play its part as the main feature here, I chose two statement plants to work as back up dancers. On the left, in a concrete planter on a wooden stand, is a large fiddle-leaf fig (*Ficus lyrata*). And on the right side, in a modern raw clay planter, a Song of India (*Dracaena reflexa*). The heights and foliage textures of these two plants play off each other perfectly. Resisting the temptation to fill the area with plants allows the space to breathe and the light to dance through the room.

In the living room, I decided to use vertical space as well as the tabletops and floor. On the metal grille that aligns with the stairwell to create a partition between the kitchen and living area, I hung mounted plants using metal "S" hooks.

SOFTLY MINIMAL
Shawn and Anne's dining room is walled with glass on three sides, making it an ideal setting for plants. While my personal style leans far toward the lush end of the spectrum, I also love a space that's minimally styled. Here, all the dining room needed was a juicy green fiddle-leaf fig (*Ficus lyrata*) and an exuberant Song of India (*Dracaena reflexa*)—just enough greenery to place an exclamation mark on the design.

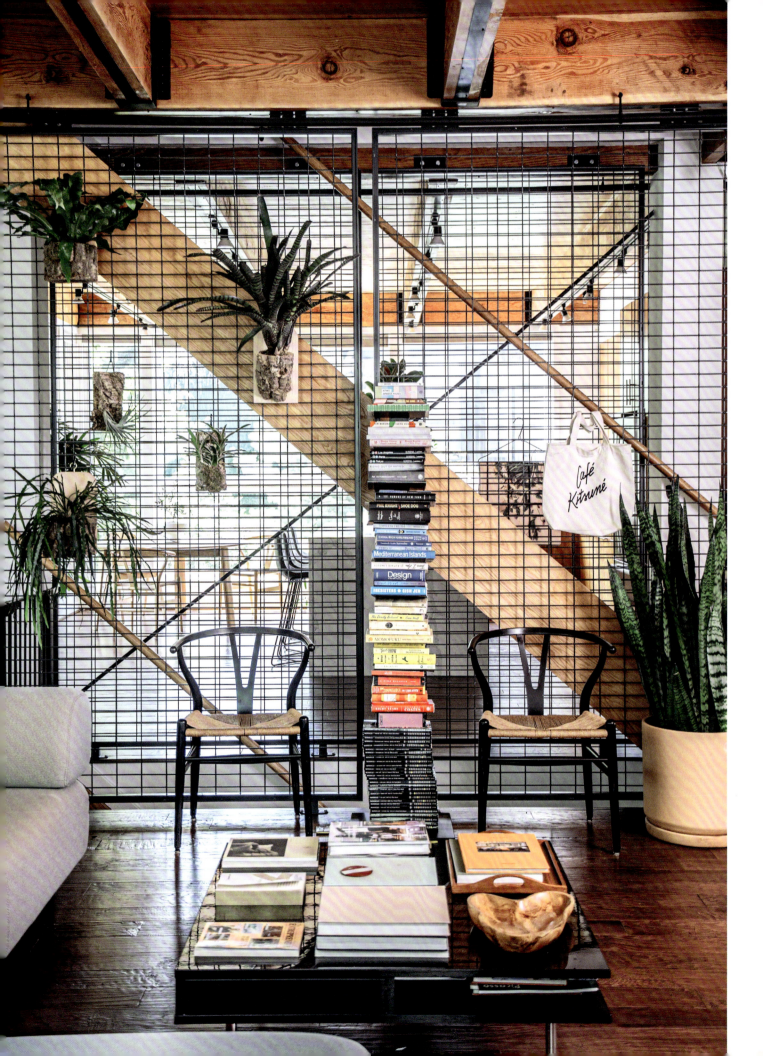

Ribbon ferns (*Pteris cretica*) and crocodile ferns (*Microsorum musifolium* 'Crocodyllus', air plants and bromeliads (*Neoregelia* 'Hannibal Lector' and 'Bossa Nova') strike a pose against the metal grid. In front stands a large snake plant (*Sansevieria trifasciata* 'Futura Robusta') in a clay planter—again, the warm clay tone was chosen to create a connection with all the wood in the home. The snake plant works well here because in a high-traffic area it's best to opt for plants that grow up, rather than out. On the sideboard across the room, I placed a Chinese evergreen (*Aglaonema*) and an N'Joy pothos (*Epipremnum aureum* N'Joy), with a braided money tree (*Pachira aquatica*) on the floor alongside.

BRINGING LIFE

The black metal grille that serves a divider between the living room, stairwell and kitchen brings an industrial vibe. To soften the feel, I hung it with mounted plants from black metal hooks (opposite). As the living room receives less light, I styled the sideboard with plants that can tolerate lower light levels—there's an N'Joy pothos and a Chinese evergreen plus a money tree alongside.

SLEEPING BEAUTIES
In Shawn and Anne's bedroom, a luxuriant *Rhaphidophora tetrasperma* is as delicate and graceful as the sheer curtains it sits between (this page). When styling a nightstand, I never want to make it too busy. Here a *Dracaena fragrans* (Demerensis Group) 'Lemon Lime' is tucked nicely in the corner (opposite above). The fluffy China doll plant (*Radermachera sinica*) is a great counterpart to hard surfaces (opposite below left). Mirrors help bounce light back into dark corners (opposite below right).

Anne and Shawn's bedroom occupies the top floor. Here, in a terra-cotta planter against the windows, I placed a *Rhaphidophora tetrasperma*, or mini monstera—I love its delicate, graceful beauty. For the nightstands, I wanted plants that wouldn't take up much space. On the right side is a *Dracaena fragrans* (Deremensis Group) 'Lemon Lime', while on the left is a ZZ plant (*Zamioculcas zamiifolia*). My final touch was a China doll plant (*Radermachera sinica*) tucked in beside the armchair. Its feathery foliage adds a little softness and blends with the greenery outside the windows.

A GATHERED SPACE

"What's in a name?". Shakespeare wrote that line in one of his most famous plays, *Romeo & Juliet*. He was questioning whether a rose would smell like a rose if it had another name. It's debatable. Does a tree make a sound when it falls in the woods if there's no one there to hear it? That's the question I have. And what does all that have to do with the boutique hotel Revival Baltimore?

Well, when a hotel is named Revival, there's intention in that. The hotel is being brought back to life. Revived! But whence does thou cometh? Sorry—Shakespeare still on the brain. What I meant to say was, what exactly is being revived? The answer is a private mansion that later became the Peabody Court Hotel, which was then renovated and opened in 2018 as Revival Baltimore. Located in Mount Vernon, one of the most sophisticated and historical neighborhoods in the city, the hotel was not only revived in its own right, but also added a much-needed sense of renewal to the neighborhood. Now it was my job to bring Revival Baltimore some added life.

I wanted to give Revival's lobby an energy that would make a lasting impression on all the guests that passed through. Jason Bass, the Director of Culture and Impact at the hotel, told me that he wanted guests to feel that they are "coming home" and the addition of plants could only help to achieve this. I mean, what's a home without plants? Shakespeare didn't ask that, but I do. Can you even call a house a home if it doesn't have plants? I don't think so. I'd go so far as to say that a life without plants is a life not fully lived. But don't let this fool you into believing the lobby wasn't stylish without plants. It was. But perhaps it was lacking in the warm feeling of "home" that it has now that it's all planted up.

I'D GO SO FAR AS TO SAY THAT A LIFE WITHOUT PLANTS IS A LIFE NOT FULLY LIVED.

So where do you find your inspiration when walking into a hotel lobby? Because it's definitely not sold at the gift shop. Actually, I take that back. When I strolled through Revival's gift store, they were selling my second book, *Wild Interiors*, so I stand corrected. One can indeed purchase inspiration there. Before I move forward, know that right there and then I did a little wink, as if to say "damn right!". OK, back to finding inspiration. Well, when I enter a space, I find inspiration everywhere. In the colors of the walls, the shapes and textures of the furniture, the artwork, the height of the ceilings, the finish of the surfaces, and, of course, the quality of the light. But which of these stands out and provides the spark? It's that spark that guides my hand when I add greenery, so the results are seamless and delicate, not heavy handed.

The Revival lobby is divided into three sections, with the front and back sections mimicking each other in their decor and styling, yet defining their differences through their function and mood. Sandwiched in between is a seating area. While the three areas have their own individual appeal, I looked at each as part of a whole, just as I did when designing my own home. While each room forms part of the same body, they must all work individually too. But when the body needs to move, all the parts move together. I use the same sense of natural flow to work in plants from room to room.

The first part of the lobby is what I call the library. It's styled with a long sectional couch and floral-patterned throw pillows in keeping with the building's Victorian style, a leather accent chair, and leather stools that nestle up to a couple of hexagonal wood coffee tables. There's also a run of vintage bookshelves, and a large wooden desk. I found my "spark" for plant styling this room in the mural on the wall. While the main feature is a large blue peacock, the majority of the walls are painted to resemble a blue sky with a wash of hazy clouds drifting through.

Taking this as my inspiration, I planned blue planters on the coffee tables and, to move the eye across the room, a blue planter on the windowsill. Two white ceramic planters were added to the side tables. Here the delicate foliage popular in the Victorian period sprang to mind, and I potted up a polka dot begonia (*Begonia maculata*) and a crocodile fern (*Microsorum musifolium* 'Crocodyllus'), both plants adding a pop of green-patterned foliage to the center of the room. On the side tables are a rabbit's foot fern (*Davallia solida* var. *fejeensis*) and a silver lace fern (*Pteris ensiformis*). Next, I placed a tall fabian aralia (*Polyscias* 'Fabian') in a blue pot on the windowsill. With its vertical growth, this sits high above the chair in front, bringing presence to the corner.

But some might say I'm leaving the best till last. Because probably the first thing that grabs your attention when you walk into the lobby of the hotel will be either the large neon pothos (*Epipremnum aureum* 'Neon') totem or the huge *Philodendron selloum*. The former stands about 7ft/2.1m in height and is dressed in a molten-gold effect

AVAILABLE ROOM
The lobby of Revival Baltimore has a relaxed feeling that aims to make guests feel right at home. In the library area of the lobby seen here, I styled a majestic *Philodendron selloum* in a modern terra-cotta planter on top of a glazed wooden cabinet. While in most scenarios a plant this size would be styled on the floor, the space and light above the cabinet makes it the perfect spot for such an imposing presence. The philodendron's shiny long-fingered foliage draws the eye from all angles and screens this space from the adjacent living room area (opposite).

A GATHERED SPACE

planter. I chose the pothos because I needed a plant that wouldn't grow horizontally and block the walkway and the first thing that popped into my head was a climbing plant. My thinking is that over time its vines will climb up the post and then can be trained to grow along the ceiling. Since pothos are tolerant of lower light levels, setting it here, about 10ft/3m from the closest window, works fine. While the plant will tolerate this exposure, it won't thrive in it, which will keep its growth under control. But which pothos to go for? In this situation, it all boiled down to color. It had to be the Neon, as I wanted something that would pop against the muted blues and grays of the walls.

On top of the adjacent bookcase, I placed a sprawling *Philodendrum selloum* that looks as if it has just been torn straight out of the wild. What I love about this plant is the way it transforms a space, instantly transporting you to a tropical destination. I dressed it a large modern terra-cotta planter that would keep it healthy and placed a gold-rimmed tray underneath. The warm terra-cotta pulls together

the earthy colors of the leather chairs, while the gold-rimmed tray picks up on the gold planter of the pothos. This mature beauty will gradually stretch its graceful foliage into the library on one side and the seating area on the other, which is up a short flight of stairs.

I decided this central space was the living room, as relaxing seems to be the main activity here. But, unlike your own home where you have just a few individuals moving from room to room, the lobby of a hotel is a bustling space. To keep the greenery out of the way while still allowing it to make an impact, all of the plants here either sit on top of furniture or are placed out of the way in a corner. Guests can come and go as they please while soaking up the lushness around them.

PLANT CONCIERGE

A quiet moment at the concierge desk with a fabian aralia (*Polyscias* 'Fabian') bringing a splash of plant life to this corner (above). Its upward growth habit makes it ideal for limited spaces like this windowsill perch. Seen from another angle, the *Philodendron selloum* perfectly balances the neon pothos totem (*Epipremnum aureum* 'Neon') sitting to the right of the staircase. The gold planter and the philodendron's base tray play off the subtle yet glamorous gold accents that are dotted around the lobby (above left).

A GATHERED SPACE

AS YOU KNOW, I'M A HUGE FAN OF PLACING PLANTS ON PEDESTALS, WHICH ELEVATES THEM TO A WORK OF ART.

QUIET MOMENTS

The ash wood pedestal was custom-made by Area Fabrication to add texture and impact to this tranquil corner. A *Philodendron* 'Imperial Green' sits on top, styled in a fluted planter that contrasts beautifully with the swirls of the wood grain (left). A detail of a delicate silver lace fern (*Pteris ensiformis*) on a side table (top left). A crocodile fern (*Microsorum musifolium* 'Crocodyllus') in a ribbed blue glazed planter brings subtle color to a coffee table in the living room (above). A peek into the living room of the lobby that welcomes all guests "home" (opposite).

With the outsize philodendron sitting above one of the couches here and creating a canopy for anyone sitting below it, I wanted to balance the heights of the other plants in this space. I commissioned a local artist to make a pedestal out of ash wood and placed it between two couches. As you know, I'm a huge fan of placing plants on pedestals, which elevates them to a piece of art (see The Art of the Pedestal, pages 48–51). But I didn't want any old pedestal. I had in mind something light-colored and raw in texture, which would not only complement the other wooden pieces in the room, but also offer tactile contrast to the modern metal lamp that stood beside it. For the work of art that would sit on top, I chose a Philodendron 'Imperial Green' and placed it in a fluted white glazed terra-cotta planter. The lush, shiny foliage of this variety picks up the glossy green subway tile that covers a nearby wall. Philodendrons are known to be great indoor plants, and this one is right at the top of my list.

On each of the two coffee tables here, I placed a glazed terra-cotta planter, one holding a Goeppertia orbifolia and the other an Anthurium 'Jungle Bush'. The positioning is ideal—these plants enjoy medium light and the glazed planters help to maintain the moisture level of the soil while harmonizing with the leather chairs nearby. At the far end of the room, beside the tile wall, I needed something that could anchor the corner without detracting from the art on the wall. So I placed a bird of paradise (Strelitzia reginae) here, where it can luxuriate in the morning sun, and chose a planter that tones with the greens of the artwork above. With all this talk of plants anchoring areas of the room, let's not forget the heavy lifting that smaller plants do. On a black wooden buffet at the end of this space stands a model of the hotel. To create a cool moment, I put a parlor palm (Chamaedorea elegans) on either side to resemble palm trees.

In the entryway across the room, I positioned two snake plants (Dracaena trifasciata) in concrete planters. I felt there needed to be some greenery here to greet guests as they come in and out, but as this area is so far from the windows, low-light-tolerant plants were necessary. When styling entryways, staircases, or hallways, I'll often work in a vertical-growing snake plant, dracaena, or aralia.

A "LIVING" ROOM

This model of Revival inspired me to place a small parlor palm (*Chamaedorea elegans*) either side of it, creating a fun little diorama (left). A detail of an *Anthurium* 'Jungle Bush' that sits on a coffee table (above left and opposite). A compact *Philodendron* 'Birkin' styled in a ribbed yellow planter adds a splash of warm color to the far side of the room (above). This area of the lobby has a warm and inviting vibe that entices guests to take a seat. The wooden ceiling, green tile wall, and leather furniture all chime with the lush greenery to create a true "living" room.

Finishing off the lobby is an area that I call the quiet place—you might find guests there chatting or catching up on work. Accordingly, I wanted to bring in plants that created a tranquil mood. On either side of the room, in white glazed clay planters, I placed two small *Philodendron* 'McColley's Finale', while on the coffee tables ribbed planters hold a *Philodendron* 'Birkin' and a crocodile fern (*Microsorum musifolium* 'Crocodyllus'). To reinforce the idea of tranquility, and make an unforgettable statement, I positioned an 8-ft/2.4-m Norfolk Island pine (*Araucaria heterophylla*) in the center of the room. These wispy, graceful trees remind me of the "great outdoors." And when I think of that, what comes to mind is the chill in the air, the sounds of wildlife, and the smell of pine, of course. Not only is this tree the perfect conversation starter, come winter and the holidays, it is also the perfect tree to decorate. So I ask the question again: if this tree falls in the lobby and there are no guests to hear it, does it make a sound?

BIG STATEMENT, QUIET SPACE
In a quiet part of the lobby, I positioned a lofty Norfolk Island pine (*Araucaria heterophylla*) in the center of a seating area—it creates a bold centerpiece for the space. The pine's sheltering presence draws guests to gather around it (left). A *Philodendron* 'McColley's Finale' sits in a glazed white planter on a side table (above).

A GATHERED SPACE

UNTITLED
(THE PAINTER AND THE PHOTOGRAPHER)

What happens when you put two talented artists in a house together? Well, clearly their love and creativity will be expressed through the items they bring together to create their home. A better way to put that might be to say that their home becomes a joint artistic project or statement. Maybe that's a little dramatic, but when discussing the home of painter Cindy Daignault and photographer Curran Hatleberg, I need to stand on a table to give voice to my feelings. Or I can just write them down right here in this book for you to read.

In their newly renovated, mid-century modern home, tucked into a lush corner of Baltimore, Cindy and Curran have created an interior that is full of warmth and infused with a sense of authenticity and exploration. Every single piece here has been placed with thought and purpose. But, of course, I wouldn't expect anything less from the home of two artists.

In many of the homes that I visit, I find there's one partner in charge of the plant care and another who is there purely for the feel-good plant vibes. And that was the situation here. When I first met Cindy— the main plant nurturer in the family—she requested that I make the rooms that already contained plants feel more organized and styled, and help make the rooms without plants a touch greener.

Cindy, a true plant-lover, understands the power that plants have in transforming the look and feel of a space and how their presence affects those that live alongside them. She has been collecting plants over the years but, due to her busy schedule, has never had enough time to track down exactly the right pots and arrangements to fit the aesthetic of her home. So, therein lay my challenge—a challenge I accepted without hesitation, because as a plant stylist, this is where my own sense of creativity comes into play.

When working with artists, there's always a slight feeling of nervousness because I want everything to look just right and for all the pieces to mesh perfectly with the home owners' aesthetic. Cindy and Curran evidently love color, texture, pattern, and mid-century style, so I decided to use these elements as inspiration for the plants I would bring in and the planters in which I'd style them.

When you walk into this home, a long hallway leads to an open-plan kitchen, dining, and living room. With three key rooms combined in one large space, it makes sense that this would be the area with the most plants. It also has the most natural light, thanks to large glass sliding doors running the entire length of the space. When styling a home, I usually give each room its own theme and work plants and planters in accordingly, but when working with a large open-plan space like this one, I look at it as a whole. What helps here is that Cindy and Curran have styled the space cohesively, repeating the same colors, textures, and mid-century furnishings throughout.

I WANTED EACH NEW PLANT TO BE SPECIAL, AS IF I WAS GIFTING CINDY AND CURRAN NEW FRIENDS.

My starting point was distributing plants evenly throughout the space to create a sense of visual balance. The couple already owned four large mature plants that needed a little help in terms of presentation: a large Swiss cheese plant (*Monstera deliciosa*), an umbrella plant (*Schefflera*), a fiddle-leaf fig (*Ficus lyrata*), and a Norfolk Island pine (*Araucaria heterophylla*). The Swiss cheese plant needed repotting and its vines had grown long, snaking their way along the floor. I chose to style it in a modern terra-cotta planter and added a tall wooden stake to train the vines upward. This helped move the foliage out of the walkway and gave the plant more presence in the room. The fiddle-leaf fig was bushy and overgrown, so it needed to be trained into a shape that was tall rather than wide. However, there was no need to repot it, because the planter had developed a gorgeous patina, mimicking the look of the wood grain in the walnut features that are woven throughout this space. That's the beauty of aged terra-cotta. Over time, moisture repeatedly dries and builds up on the pot, creating an attractive weathered look that chimes perfectly with some styles of decor. The umbrella plant had the same issues as the fiddle, but in this instance I decided to repot it in a new ceramic planter with a wooden stand, of a kind that was popular in the mid-20th century. Last but not least, the Norfolk Island pine just needed to be shown off to its full advantage.

I wanted each new plant to be special, as if I was gifting Cindy and Curran new friends. As the room was already home to several large specimens, I chose a variety of medium- and smaller-size plants to cluster around them, many of which have interesting variations of color and texture in their foliage. As a centerpiece on the dining room table, I chose an *Alocasia cuprea* and dressed it in a *nerikomi*-style planter that harmonizes perfectly with the rugs in the room. On top of the buffet separating the dining table from the living area, I positioned a *Philodendron squamicaule* in a terra-cotta pot. Such a rare beauty deserves to be the center of attention. Beside the buffet, styled in a pale orange mid-century modern planter, a *Philodendron* 'Painted Lady', adds a pop of color and texture between the buffet and the neighboring couch (I loved the idea of introducing a 'Painted Lady' to an artist's home). The pale orange planter works perfectly with the reddish-orange stems of the newly unfurled 'Painted Lady' leaves.

To the right of the buffet I styled a *Dracaena marginata* 'Tarzan' in a black planter. This added a mid-range height to the plants in the room. The exquisite bar cubby is occupied by a small *Ficus triangularis* in a gray planter. I wanted to add a splash of plant life to this nook, but didn't want anything that would get in the way of cocktail making. Lastly, below the Swiss cheese plant, I tucked a China doll plant (*Radermachera sinica*) in a white brutalist-style planter.

PICTURE PERFECT
With an open floorplan, it's important to link each area to the next. In Cindy and Curran's home, these links are created with a wonderful mix of textures, colors, patterns, and shapes. With a great collection of plants and vintage pieces, their home is truly picture-perfect (opposite).

WIDE FORMAT
In the dining area, mismatched chairs and a live-edge wood table sit on a rug that weaves together a rich mix of colors. To complement all of the goodness happening around and below the table, I styled an *Alocasia cuprea* in a custom *nerikomi*-style planter by Pamela Zhang as the centerpiece. With large windows along both sides of the room, the light in this area increases the options for the types of plants that can be styled here.

WELL BALANCED

Dracaena marginata 'Tarzan' stands tall in a modern black planter to create a sense of separation between the dining and living spaces (left). The full, bushy growth of the plant balances the weight of the outsize *Monstera deliciosa* on the other side of the room. The rare *Philodendron squamicaule* shines bright as the statement plant on the buffet (below left). Looking from the dining area into the kitchen, Cindy and Curran's love of natural materials is evident. Thanks to the slatted walnut ceiling and marble island top and walnut base, this space feels lush even with minimal pops of greenery.

COLOR BAR

The bar cubby, lined in rich walnut, is one of my favorite details in this incredible home. The warm lighting, the bottle labels, the woven cloth, and the small *Ficus triangularis* with its unique triangle-shaped leaves make for an enticing vignette (left). The living area is encircled by Cindy and Curran's large mature plants and continues the earthy natural vibe of the kitchen and dining room (below).

UNTITLED (THE PAINTER AND THE PHOTOGRAPHER)

BOLD STROKES
In the bedroom, I wanted the plants and planters to fit seamlessly with the bold strokes of color in the Nigerian beaded chair and the rug (below and opposite below right). The artwork "Untitled (The Show is Over)" by Felix Gonzalez-Torres in conjunction with Christopher Wool, sits next to a gold dust croton on a clear acrylic pedestal and the pothos *Epipremnum pinnatum* 'Cebu Blue' (opposite above left). *Ficus benghalensis* 'Audrey' is starting to reach out and form a canopy over the bed (opposite above right).

I wanted something soft and delicate peeking out from beneath the large, jungly foliage of the *Monstera deliciosa* and this fitted the bill perfectly.

Cindy and Curran's bedroom boasts bright colors and wild patterns in the shape of a rug and accent chair. To add to the sense of fun, I styled the side table with an *Alocasia sinuata* in a blue geometric planter and a *Peperomia caperata* 'Emerald Ripple' in a yellow planter. I actually picked out the planters before the plants, because I wanted something that would dance well with the chair and rug. Once I knew the planters I was rolling with, I looked for plants to complement them—the rippled foliage of these two pairs so well with the layered style of the planters. To the right of the chair, I added a *Dracaena fragrans* (Deremensis Group) 'Lemon Lime' to reference the vines in the pattern of the chair.

The nightstand closest to the side window seemed the right spot for a medium-size banyan (*Ficus benghalensis* 'Audrey') in a modern glazed black planter. I wanted to give the bed a little canopy of sorts and add some height to the banyan, so on the other side of the room, next to the windows, I stacked a gold dust croton (*Codiaeum variegatum* 'Gold Dust') in a contemporary white planter on top of a transparent pedestal, while below it the blue-green foliage of pothos *Epipremnum pinnatum* 'Cebu Blue' trails gracefully down to the floor.

UNTITLED (THE PAINTER AND THE PHOTOGRAPHER)

BATHROOM BEAUTIES
A terrarium in a sleek, tulip-shaped glass vase sits on the bathroom windowsill (left). Below the shower window, I styled a large Australian tree fern, a lemon button fern, and a rabbit's foot fern (below left and opposite above right). A flourishing air plant wreath hangs on the back wall of the shower (opposite above left). This little group of humidity lovers are bathing in the moisture-rich bathroom atmosphere (opposite below right). A variegated Boston fern and *Epipremnum pinnatum* Marble Planet perch on top of the towel rack (opposite below left).

The main bathroom gave me the opportunity to pull out some moisture-loving favorites. The countertop is home to a small glass terrarium, a jade bonsai (*Portulacaria afra*), and a *Maranta leuconeura* var. *erythroneura* 'Lemon Lime', while on the top shelf of the towel rack you'll find a variegated Boston fern (*Nephrolepis exaltata* 'Tiger Fern') and a *Epipremnum pinnatum* Marble Planet in glazed terra-cotta planters. The shower has a floor-to-ceiling window with woodland views, so to blur the boundaries between inside and out, I added a small grouping of plants at the floor of the shower. I chose an Australian tree fern (*Dicksonia antarctica*) in a terra-cotta colored pot, a lemon button fern (*Nephrolepis duffii*) in a geometric blue planter, and a rabbit's foot fern (*Davallia solida* var. *fejeensis*) potted in cork. While these ferns will luxuriate in the steamy moisture of the shower, they are out of reach of the hot and cold spray. My final touch was to hang an air plant (*Tillandsia*) wreath in the center of the shower.

When I see how this space came together, I feel that I've added a little extra layer of goodness. As a child, my mother would always tell me to leave a place better than I found it. And although it would be hard to leave a home like this "better" than I found it, I can honestly say I left it looking much greener, more luscious, and well-styled. I guess it could be said that this is my artist's statement.

STYLING A CHILD'S ROOM

CHOOSING AND STYLING THE RIGHT PLANTS FOR CUTE KIDS' SPACES

If the kitchen is the heart of the home, then surely a child's room must be the imagination. And there is so much that can be done to capture the imagination of a child when styling their room. A child's own space should be cozy, colorful, and, of course, cute. Let's be honest—if it's going to be anything, it should definitely be cute. But more than this, a young person's mind should be encouraged to explore and run wild within their room. The books, the toys, the wallpaper and artworks that grace the walls—creating a little world for your little ones is so important, and it also brings a great deal of joy to a parent.

As with every other room in the home, the addition of plants to a nursery or child's room will change the mood and bring benefits to those that dwell alongside them. But of course you want to keep your little angels safe. So when plant styling a child's room, it's essential to avoid any plants that might be dangerous for kids to touch or ingest. Instead, look for fun ways to introduce plants that are child-friendly. On the following pages, you'll find some of my favorite techniques and tips when styling a child's room with plants.

CREATING JOYFUL SPACES

MY HEART
Teaching Holland to be gentle with our plants has been one of my biggest challenges, but I see how she watches me tend to them and can't wait until she's able to join in (opposite). Small air plants are styled in two glazed ceramic animal planters (below). With only a few live plants in Holland's nursery, we relied on the mural, painted by Drury Bynum, to set the tone (right).

A couple of years ago, if you'd asked me about styling a nursery, I would have immediately pictured somewhere you go to purchase young plants and trees. But nowadays when I'm asked the same question, my mind goes directly to my daughter's room. Her nursery. Recently I became a father to a beautiful baby girl and since the day she arrived I've been an emotional mess. I've cried without warning, smiled until my face ached, and slept...oh yeah, I haven't slept. By the time this book is published, I will be the father of a 20-month-old baby girl named Holland. Actually, if this book ever comes out, it'll be a miracle because...I'm the father of a new little human. I mean I've propagated plants before but a whole human?!

So when it came to designing the perfect room for our little angel, I needed to make it magical. Of course, we picked out the color of the paint for the walls to set the right tone and took the opportunity to have the artist Drury Bynum (who worked with me on the Jungle by Numbers project in *Wild Creations*) paint a mural of a lush jungle and mystical creatures on the wall. Fiona and I worked hard to find all the furniture, drapes, and decor that would make the room come together, but once everything was set in place, I felt there was something missing. And, of course, that "something" was plants.

Holland's room has two windows, one facing north and the other facing west, both shaded by a large pine tree that sits directly outside, limiting the available light here as well as my options for choosing plants. Luckily, many plants that tolerate lower light exposure are nontoxic to humans. Now, you might be wondering why I'm bringing up the

CREATING JOYFUL SPACES

COZY CORNERS
In Holland's room, I styled a cozy corner for reading surrounded by kid-friendly greenery. A little group of moisture-lovers includes a polka dot begonia and an open terrarium (opposite above left). A spider plant is a great choice for a kid's room (opposite above right). A parlor palm creates a pop of green against the mural (opposite below right).

"nontoxic" part here. You're saying to yourself, "Huh? Why does it matter if a plant is nontoxic or not? I'm not planning to eat it." And no, of course you're not…but an infant or toddler is a different matter. Anything that they can pick up or grab or push their adorable little faces into will make its way into their mouths. So—and I cannot emphasize this strongly enough—when you have plants in a room that a young child sleeps or plays in, it is of the utmost importance that those plants will not cause any harm if and when ingested.

In most situations, I'm looking to create luxuriant moments in a room, but when working on a kid's room I limit the number of plants I introduce. For Holland's room, I chose to place a few small air plants in ceramic animal holders on a shelf. Having fun with the planters in a kid's room can give the space a childlike energy and playfulness that you don't typically see with plant design. Air plants are great as they don't require soil, so you're limiting the opportunity for mess. They will also bloom when given the right care and everyone enjoys seeing that fresh pop of color unfurl into the room. At the opposite end of the shelf, I potted a polka dot begonia (*Begonia maculata*) in a cranberry colored planter and a fern grouping in a clear pot. For the begonia, I chose that color planter because it plays well with the red hues on the underside of the begonia's foliage and the color of the walls. Not only is the polka dot begonia safe for kids, but also its spotty leaves really grab their attention and help get them excited about plants and plant care.

ANIMAL WILD

When styling a kid's room, I like to bring plants into the vertical space, either hanging them from the ceiling or mounting them on the wall. This keeps the plants away from little fingers yet brings a touch of life to the room. Children have such a wonderful natural sense of curiosity, and introducing plants that encourage that excitement is everything, especially when a plant is reminiscent of a familiar animal. One of my favorite child-friendly plants is the staghorn fern (*Platycerium bifurcatum*). Given its name because its foliage resembles the antlers of a stag, you can easily understand why it's a hit with kids. The connection helps a child create a bond with the plant, so don't be surprised if he or she dreams up some interesting nicknames for their new plant friend. When mounted on a wall, a staghorn fern creates a punch of wilderness bursting into the room.

As shown in *Living Walls* (see pages 32—37) there are many plants that can be mounted on a wall. Some of the others that I would suggest for a child's room are the crocodile fern (*Microsorum musifolium* 'Crocodyllus'), the rabbit foot fern (*Davallia solida* var. *fejeensis*), and air plants (*Tillandsia*). Crocodile ferns are perfect for a kid's room because, just like the staghorn, they are nontoxic and, as their name suggests, they have leathery, bright green foliage that resembles the hide of a crocodile.

PLANT PLAYTIME
Cindy Daignault and Curran Hatleberg's son River loves a spot of indoor camping. In his adorable room, I styled a *Goeppertia orbifolia* in a white clay planter to add a little greenery to his campsite. In the room of John Makowski and Bridget Weininger's son, Johnny, I styled a staghorn fern mounted on cork, next to his shelves of toys (opposite right). While the ZZ plant (*Zamioculcas zamiifolia*) is toxic, you should have no concerns using it in an older child's room (opposite left).

RIVER WILD

A cluster of plants in the corner of River's room (above). I've styled a *Sansevieria sayuri*, a staghorn fern, and a small *Geogenanthus*. A staghorn fern potted in cork and mounted on wood hangs in the window (above right). On top of River's coat rack, I've styled a *Peperomia obtusifolia* 'Variegata' in a sloth planter to balance the cuteness of the fawn lamp (right). I don't think I've ever been jealous of a kid's room before, but I must admit that Cindy and Curran went all the way with styling River's room. So much color and life are spread throughout the room (opposite).

LITTLE GLASS JUNGLES

The magic a terrarium can bring is endless. In almost every kid's room I've ever styled, I have left them with a little glass jungle to add a dash of whimsy to their space. Obviously, kids' rooms tend to be created by adults. So when creating a terrarium, you have the opportunity to add something that will spark the imagination of the child who occupies that room, and inspire an interest in and appreciation for that terrarium and its contents. (See my book *Wild Creations* for how to create the perfect terrarium.)

PREHISTORIC GOODNESS
In Johnny's room, I styled a terrarium with a mix of maidenhair ferns, a watermelon begonia, and polka dot begonia (above). Whenever I style a space with plants, I do a walkthrough first to get an idea of what the individuals who live there are into. Seeing that Johnny loved dinosaurs, I worked small figurines into the terrarium (above right). Using figures to make plants fun for kids is also fun for those styling them (right).

There are many types of fun glass or plastic vessels that can be used to create a terrarium. My favorites are enclosed terrariums, because they create their own ecosystem and so require much less care as they do not need watering. An enclosed terrarium can be a mini-glasshouse style, a jar with a cork top, or, if you're feeling wild, a fillable lamp. Plant up these little worlds of wonder with ferns, calatheas, anthuriums, alocasias, or peperomias. The finishing touch is the addition of tiny figurines. From small wilderness creatures to prehistoric giants, such figures make these little glass jungles come to life in a way children truly enjoy, no matter what their age.

INTO THE WILD

For my goddaughter Sienna's desk, I turned a fillable glass lamp base into a terrarium and added a cheery *Peperomia albovittata* in a snail planter for a touch of fun. Shawn and Anne Chopra's son Avi will enjoy this little jungle diorama with its friendly bear for years to come (left and below).

LITTLE GLASS JUNGLES 209

PLAYFUL PLANTERS

The world of playful planters can be endless, and when styling a kid's room you can have a lot of fun looking for planters that capture a child's imagination and suit the vibe of the space. Just as I interview my clients to get an idea of who they are and what they like before bringing plants into their spaces, I like to meet the kids to understand what types of plants and planters will spark joy.

There are so many bright colorful planters and simple designs that will add a pop of color to a corner but won't detract from the attractiveness of the plants inside them. You could go with planters designed to resemble animals, fun foods, or even cartoon characters which tap into whatever that child might be into at that moment. Sometimes for older kids, it's the cool shape of a planter that makes the difference. The idea here is to get adventurous with your choice of planters, because there's always room for more awesome in a child's life.

MOSSY ART

Not every space has the right quality of light for plant life, so finding creative ways to add greenery is key. In most kid spaces, this can be done by covering the walls in a jungle-print wallpaper. This immediately adds plant detailing and energy to a kid's room, but what about the art on the walls? Just as a mounted staghorn fern creates a 3D installation on the wall, hanging moss art will do the same, and without demanding a good light source or any watering.

While it's possible to purchase artwork made with preserved moss, you can also do it yourself at home, as a fun activity with your kids (take a look at my book *Wild Creations* for how to create moss art). There are many different colors and textures of preserved moss, so you're sure to find what you need to create a work of art that fits perfectly with the look of the room.

YOUNG, COLORFUL, AND WILD
Styling a child's room is an opportunity to go wild with color, shape, and the unexpected. Quirky and fun planters suit the playful, lighthearted vibe (opposite). If there's a spot that doesn't enjoy a lot of light, using moss art to brighten it works wonders (this page).

PLANTS FOR KIDS' SPACES

AIR PLANTS
(TILLIANDSIA)

Seems like many folk find air plants mystical and difficult to care for. I believe the reason people believe they are hard to keep alive is down to their name—"air" plant—which suggests that they only get their water from the air. Out in the wild that may be the case, but at home you'll need to do a little more work for them to love you.

Like staghorn ferns, fishbone cacti, or orchids, air plants are epiphytes, which means they are plants that grow on other plants, and in their natural habitats you'll find them clinging to shrubs, bushes, and trees. As air plants are nontoxic, they can provide a great sprinkle of greenery in a nursery, older kid's room, or anywhere in the home.

STYLING TIPS As air plants grow on trees in the wild, try styling them as if from a tree in your child's room. Plant them in hanging vessels and dangle them near a crib to create a living mobile or try creating an air plant wreath (see my book *Wild Creations* for instructions).

LIGHT Air plants can thrive anywhere from bright indirect light to indirect light, but the brighter, the better. That doesn't mean direct sunlight though—that will cause them to wilt and dry up quickly. The cute and curly *Tillandsia streptophylla* air plant is the rare exception that can tolerate a little direct sun.

WATER When it comes to growing tillandsias, it's a case of recreating the plants' natural habitat, so the more humidity you can provide, the better. Make sure to mist and soak them in a lukewarm bath weekly. We often have a humidifier running in our daughter's nursery and air plants just love this.

TEMPERATURE Keep air plants in a cool spot between 60–80°F/15–27°C but away from the direct draft of air conditioners or heaters.

PROPAGATION Propagate air plants using the division and separation method. They will grow new pups on their sides as the plant matures. Once these pups are about a third the size of the mother plant, they can be separated from the mother by gently pulling at the base.

CALATHEA
(WHITE FUSION)

Just like the rest of the *Calathea* family, 'White Fusion' is admired due to its bold and beautiful foliage. Its variegated markings resemble a marbling of white into green, while a bright fuchsia underbelly runs down the stem. Their colors are one of the reasons I love to style calatheas in kids' rooms and the fact that they are nontoxic makes them an easy addition.

STYLING TIPS Calatheas need to stay on the moist side, so styling them in glazed ceramic or plastic pots is ideal. They tend to grow smaller indoors, so grouping them next to other plants makes them more impactful. Try pairing them with similar plants, such as *Calathea setosa* or the rattlesnake plant (*Goeppertia orbifolia*).

LIGHT Calatheas are very forgiving when it comes to most light situations in a room. To keep the variegation of 'White Fusion' developing in new growth, make sure it is placed in bright but indirect light. While the plant will tolerate lower light, you'll start to see the white in the foliage slowly fade away and become replaced by more green. Avoid placing 'White Fusion' in south- or west-facing windows.

WATER Keeping the soil evenly moist is key to the health of this plant. So while calatheas may give you a break when it comes to light, they are very demanding when it comes to moisture. Humidity is also helpful, so misting weekly or adding a humidifier into the room would be beneficial.

SOIL Wrap the roots in a soil medium that is well aerated with a mix of bark, sphagnum moss, a bit of perlite, and organic potting soil. This will help keep the soil moist for longer and help your plant thrive.

TEMPERATURE 'White Fusion' will be happy in an environment that's between 65–75°F /19–24°C during the day and no cooler than 60°F/15°C at night. Keep it out of the direct blast of air conditioners and heaters.

FISHBONE CACTUS
(EPIPHYLLUM ANGULIGER)

There are two main reasons why I love the fishbone cactus. Firstly, because it has the perfect name. Look, the plant namers were either going to go with chainsaw or fishbone, and I'm a strong lover of the latter. And secondly, it has no spines. I'm sorry, I don't think you heard me—it has no spines. So there is no danger bringing this cactus into the rooms of babes. Not only that, but it is also nontoxic, so we are doubling down with awesomeness. Oh, you want to triple down? Well, I don't mind if I do. Because fishbone cacti are epiphytic (do not root in soil) like our wonderful friend the staghorn fern, they can be mounted and placed on a wall. So many reasons to introduce a fishbone cactus into the world of a child!

STYLING TIPS As mentioned, you can mount fishbone cacti and style them as a part of a gallery wall or let them burst forth from a hanging basket. They like their soil to be slightly dry, so a porous container is best.

LIGHT The fishbone cactus absolutely loves bright indirect light. In the wild, they grow under the leaves of trees, bathing in dappled, indirect light throughout the day. Try your best to mimic that effect in your child's room.

WATER The fishbone cactus is not from the desert but from the jungles of Mexico, so they like water more than your typical cacti. I water mine when the top half of the soil is completely dry. Remember always to use lukewarm water and pour it over the soil slowly, making sure every part of the surface gets some moisture. Since fishbones are born in the jungle, treat them like tropical plants by placing them in a room with a humidifier and/or misting weekly.

SOIL Surround the fishbone's roots with free-draining, nutrient-rich soil. For most of my cacti, I like a mix of one part perlite, one part peat moss, and three parts cacti mix.

TEMPERATURE Keep fishbone cacti in a space with stable temperatures of between 60–75°F/16–24°C, making sure they never spend extended periods of time above or below that. If taking them outside during warmer periods, make sure to keep track of the day's highs and lows.

PARLOR PALM
(CHAMAEDOREA ELEGANS)

The parlor palm is the perfect plant for any room in your home, thanks to its ability to tolerate different types of light and to thrive indoors. But what makes it one of my favorites for styling is the fact that it quickly makes a space feel more lush and tropical. I mean what's a jungle without a palm tree? And what's plant styling without a parlor palm? They've been helping to blur the line of indoor and outdoor since the Victorian era. And in your home they will grow beautifully, making your space feel great and keeping you confident as a plant parent.

STYLING TIPS Easygoing and elegant, the parlor palm isn't going to grab your attention because of the look or shape of its foliage, so to help it stand out, style it in a decorative pot that makes a statement. I love the look of them in a nursery, parked beside a lounge chair.

LIGHT Find the spot that works best for the plant but also for you. Parlor palms will thrive in bright indirect light but can also tolerate low light situations. If the goal is to have it grow more slowly, keep it in lower light, but if you're looking to see it get full and bushy, then the brighter the light, the better. Avoid growing them beside south- or west-facing windows

WATER Parlor palms need a good drink when the soil is completely dry, and I use a moisture gauge to measure this. Given that these palms are native to the jungles of Mexico, providing them with good humidity will keep them happy. Adding a humidifier and misting once a week works wonders.

SOIL A mix of perlite, peat moss, and organic soil would be great. The goal is to make sure the soil doesn't hold onto moisture for too long.

TEMPERATURE Keep them between 60–80°F/15–27°C, making sure they never spend extended periods of time outside that temperature range.

BIRD'S NEST FERN
(ASPLENIUM NIDUS)

The bird's nest fern is one of my favorite ferns for a kid's room. With their rosette of crinkled fronds, they are a perfect statement plant. Another epiphyte, meaning they grow on trees in the wild like a staghorn fern, these ferns get their name from birds nesting in them. While you won't have to worry about this happening at home, I can't promise you won't find your kid taking a nap in one.

STYLING TIPS I like a stout, round pot to play off the bird's nest fern's bushy appearance. Because they are epiphytic, they look great mounted on a wall as well.

LIGHT Bird's nest ferns will thrive in bright indirect light but can tolerate medium to low light situations. Avoid placing them in direct sun from southern, and western-facing windows, as this will burn the leaves.

WATER Unlike with many other ferns, leave the top half of the soil to dry out before watering. Wet the soil slowly until the water flows out into the base tray. I prefer to bottom water these ferns by filling the base tray with water and letting the soil absorb the water through the drainage holes. Humidity is key, so mist weekly.

SOIL Wrap the roots in a soil medium that is well aerated with a mix of bark, sphagnum moss, and organic potting soil. This will help keep the soil moist for longer and ensure the plant thrives.

TEMPERATURE: These ferns will thrive between 65–75°F/19–24°C. If placing them outdoors during the warmer months, be sure to keep track of the temperature highs and lows.

SPIDER PLANT
(CHLOROPHYTUM COMOSUM)

Someone was brave when deciding to call this plant a spider plant. I mean, spiders aren't the most beloved creatures on this planet. Honestly, if there was a list of most-beloved creatures, the spider would probably be right at the very bottom, along with mosquitoes. So why name a plant after a spider? Well, it's because of the way its long, arching stems produce plantlets that dangle down from the mother plant (the web). With this name, it can be either an exciting plant to bring into a kid's world or a terrifying one. Choose wisely. Known as one of the most effective plants when it comes to purifying the air in a room, spider plants make the perfect addition to any bedroom.

STYLING TIPS Since the spider plant is mildly toxic, styling it high in a hanging planter or on a tall bookshelf is best. Try placing it in a terra-cotta or coconut-lined hanging basket and allow the leaves to cascade beautifully down into the nursery.

LIGHT The spider plant thrives in areas with bright indirect light but can also tolerate lower light conditions. The more light they have, the faster they will grow, and the lower the light levels, the slower they will grow. Like most tropical plants that grow at lower levels in their natural habitat, exposure to direct sun can cause sunburned foliage that turns crispy brown.

WATER Keep the soil slightly moist at all times by checking the moisture level with your finger or a moisture meter every few days. To prevent overwatering and and root rot, place spider plants in planters with good drainage. While spiders like their soil moist, they don't want to sit in water.

SOIL Use a nutrient-rich soil medium that is free-draining but retains enough moisture to allow the roots to pull water in.

TEMPERATURE Humid conditions will keep this plant happy, so a nursery or kid's room with a humidifer would be perfect. It will thrive where the temperature remains around 60–80°F/15–27°C.

VENUS FLYTRAP
(DIONAEA MUSCIPULA)

The Venus flytrap has been a favorite of mine since I was a child and saw the movie *The Little Shop of Horrors* for the first time. While I didn't want to get caught between the "teeth" of this carnivorous plant, I was fascinated by the way in which it captures bugs and feeds off them. In the home, they can't do all the hunting themselves—sometimes you have to help them catch a few small pests, and if you want to get rid of gnats adding a Venus flytrap could help. While I wouldn't introduce them to a toddler's room, for a child between the ages of 7 and 10 they can bring excitement, fun and education to their space.

STYLING TIPS Dress Venus flytraps in a glazed ceramic or plastic pot that has drainage but also character. Playful planters (see page 210) can make such plants more engaging for your young one. One cool way to style them is inside a terrarium.

LIGHT The Venus flytrap will thrive in bright indirect light but will suffer in direct sun. Placing them in a north- or east-facing window would be perfect.

WATER Flytraps are jungle plants that love moisture and humidity, so keep the top of the soil evenly moist but never soaking wet. It is beneficial to give them rainwater, or distilled water. I bottom water them by placing water in the base tray of the pot and letting the soil absorb the moisture through the drainage holes. During drier months, place them close to a humidifier and mist them weekly.

SOIL A combination of sphagnum moss, sand, and organic potting mix would be ideal. You want the mix to retain moisture but drain properly.

TEMPERATURE Keep flytraps in a space that remains consistently between 65–75°F/19–24°C.

RATTLESNAKE PLANT *(GOEPPERTIA INSIGNIS)*

Plants in the *Goeppertia* genus, and the similar *Calathea* genus, have the most vibrant and stylish foliage of any other group of plants out there in the world. That's just my opinion, of course, but the fact is that when you're looking to style a kid's room, these plants bring a different energy, a splash of color and a true beauty to the space. And one of my favorites in that family is the rattlesnake plant. It has long, wavy leaves that appear to be painted on the topside with a lime-green undercoat, faint strokes of dark green around the edges, and strong dotted strokes in the center. The drama sneaks in on the underside of the foliage too, which is the most incredible shade of burgundy, typical of many *Goeppertia* plants.

I love styling rattlesnake plants in kids' rooms, not only because they are nontoxic, but also due to the dance their foliage does throughout the day, opening up into a bush-like form during the day and folding up their leaves at night. While you won't see this process take place in real time, throughout the day you and your child will notice the change and that becomes a fun surprise for the child.

STYLING TIPS Since rattlesnake plants have a wider form, placing them on the floor or on a shelf would look great. Style them in glazed ceramic or plastic pots, which will help them retain moisture in their soil.

LIGHT Rattlesnake plants are forgiving when it comes to most light situations. They can tolerate low light but will be their strongest and most vibrant in bright indirect light. Avoid placing them in south- or west-facing windows as direct light will make the leaves fade.

WATER Keeping the soil evenly moist is key to the health of this plant. So while rattlesnake plants may give you a break when it comes to light, they are demanding when it comes to moisture. Humidity is helpful, so misting them weekly or adding a humidifier to the room would be beneficial.

SOIL Make sure the roots sit in a soil medium that is well aerated with a mix of bark, sphagnum moss and organic potting soil. This will keep the soil moist longer and help the plant thrive.

TEMPERATURE Place this plant in areas of your home that stay between 65–75°F/19–24°C during the day and no cooler than 60°F/15°C at night. It's best to keep it out of the direct blast of air conditioners and heaters.

TRIOSTAR STROMANTHE
(STROMANTHE SANGUINEA 'TRIOSTAR')

What kids will love about the Triostar, other than its cool nickname, is that they do a little dance throughout the day, just like calatheas. At dusk the triostar folds up its leaves into what's called a prayer position, then once day arrives it opens them up again to bathe in the light. The beautiful colors of the triostar are what make it so desirable. While the surface of the leaves displays streaks of dusty pink, cream, and deep green, the underside is a vibrant shade of pinot noir. This plant will bring color and life to a kid's room.

STYLING TIPS Since the Triostar is nontoxic to humans, when it comes to styling it you can go wild. Start by placing it in a glazed ceramic or plastic planter that will keep the soil moist. Let its colorful foliage take center stage and avoid planters with busy patterns—a simple, flat-colored pot will allow the beauty of the Triostar to shine. Thanks to its busy form, placing it on the floor in front of a grouping of plants, or on a small pedestal on its own, would be ideal.

LIGHT It's always best to place plants in the brightest source of indirect light as possible and the Triostar is no exception. It will thrive in bright indirect light but can tolerate medium light (about 5ft/1.5m away from a window). I prefer styling them a little bit away from a window because this prevents the soil from drying out too fast and keeps them out of direct sun, which can be harmful to the foliage.

WATER The Triostar is a thirsty plant. Keep the soil evenly moist by checking the top of the soil every other day to make sure it's damp to the touch. Be careful never to let it get waterlogged or completely dry out. One of the wonderful things about the Triostar is that when it is really thirsty, it'll call out to you by curling up its foliage. Once that happens, it's time to water it deeply, and straight away. This plant absolutely thrives in humidity. Mist the leaves weekly and during the drier times throughout the year, add a humidifier to the room it lives in.

SOIL Wrap the roots in a soil medium that is well aerated with a mix of bark, sphagnum moss, and organic soil. This will help keep the soil moist for longer and the plant should thrive.

TEMPERATURE Triostar will be happy in areas of your home that remain between 65–75°F/19–24°C degrees during the day and where the temperature drops no lower than 60°F/15°C at night. Keep it out of the blast of air conditioners and heaters.

STRING OF HEARTS
(CEROPEGIA WOODII)

Who could deny themselves the joy of bringing a string of hearts into their home? These gorgeous trailing vine plants are the perfect addition to a child's room because of the gentle, heart-shaped foliage that cascades down out of the pot and produces small flowers throughout spring and summer. Even if your infant did decide to take a bite out of a string of hearts, they are nontoxic, which only adds to their child-friendly charm.

STYLING TIPS Place a string of hearts in a hanging or wall planter so you can enjoy the long delicate vines. It is best styled in a ceramic or glass planter that will help retain moisture.

LIGHT Like so many indoor plants, the string of hearts thrives in bright indirect light but can tolerate medium light. Avoid low light and direct sun to limit the amount of stress you put on your plant.

WATER Keep the soil evenly moist. This means you'll be watering twice a week during spring and summer and once a week during fall and winter. Once the top 1in/2.5cm of soil is dry, water until the excess water comes out of the drainage holes. Mist weekly.

SOIL Use a soil medium that is well aerated with a mix of bark, sphagnum moss, a bit of perlite, and organic potting soil. This should keep the soil moist longer and help the plant thrive.

TEMPERATURE Keep your string of hearts in a room with a stable temperature between 65–80°F/ 18–26°C degrees.

INDEX

Page numbers in *italic* refer to the illustrations

A
agave, blue 132
Agave tequilana 132
Aglaonema 171
   A. 'Silver Bay' 110, 116, *117*, *119*, *160*
   A. 'Silver Queen' *31*
Ainslie, Adele *144*
air plants 15, 36, 171, 196, *197*, *201*, 203, 204, 212, *212*
Alma Cocina Latina, Baltimore 116, 152–61, *153–61*
Alocasia 12, 39, 58, 209
   A. cucullata 114
   A. cuprea 80–2, *81–3*, 188, *190*
   A. sinuata 195
Aloe vera 132
Anthurium 12, 39, 41, 209
   A. 'Jungle Bush' 181, *182–3*
   A. regale 50, 84–7, *84*, *86–7*
aralia: fabian 177, *179*
   Japanese *40*
   Ming *51*
Araucaria heterophylla 155, 185, *185*, 188
Area Fabrication *180*
artworks, moss 211, *211*
Asparagus setaceus 144, *144*
Asplenium nidus 216, *216*

B
Baltimore, Maryland 143, 150, 152–61, 174–85, 186
banyan 46
Bass, Jason 177
Beaucarnea recurvata 45, 57, 58, 132
begonia 40, *115*, *156*
   angel-wing 65–7, *66–7*
   polka dot 95, 177, 203, *203*, *208*
   watermelon 16, *208*
Begonia 'Argenteo-guttata' 65–7, *66–7*
   B. brevirimosa 111
   B. 'Lucerna' *111*
   B. maculata 95, 177, 203
   B. rex 'Escargot' 116
bird of paradise 15, *38*, 46, *181*
bonsai 42, 196
Bradshaw, Stephanie *40*, *43*, *44*
bromeliads 15, 36, 95, 171
Buddha's hand *114*
Burke, Tarana J. *41*
Bynum, Drury 59, 201, *201*

C
cacti 12, 26, 53, 54, *54–5*, 58
   fishbone 36, 136, *138*, 214, *214*
   orchid 40
   pencil 57
   prickly pear 57
Caladium 'Frog in a Blender' *124*
   C. lindenii 'Magnificum' 57
   C. praetermissum 'Hilo Beauty' 96–9, *97–9*
calamondin tree *28*, 29
Calathea 58, 209, 219, 220
   C. setosa 26, *72*, 73–4, *74–5*, 213
   C. 'White Fusion' 213, *213*
Campbell, Jamie 59, *61*
candelabra tree 46
Caravaggio 106
carnivorous plants 218, *218*
casters 156
centerpieces 38–41
Ceropegia woodii 221, *221*
Chamaedorea cataractarum 122, *142*, 143
   C. elegans 181, *182*, 215, *215*
   C. seifrizii 114, *116*, 155
Chamaerops humilis 45, 53
child's room 198–211, *199–211*
China doll plant 173, *173*, 188
Chinese evergreen 171, *171*
Chlorophytum comosum 217, *217*
Chopra, Shawn and Anne *42*, 162–73, *163–73*, 209
Cissus discolor 20
Citrus × *limon* 'Meyer' 39
Citrus × *macrocarpa* *28*, 29
Clavel, Baltimore, Maryland 130–6, *131–9*
Codiaeum variegatum 'Banana' 114

C. v. 'Gold Dust' 57, 88–91, *89–91*, 195, *195*
   C. v. var. *pictum* 'Petra' *142*
Coffea arabica 165, *166*
coffee plant 165, *166*
color 18–20
croton 12, 58
   banana 114
   gold dust 57, 88–91, *89–91*, 195, *195*
Ctenanthe oppenheimiana 'Amagris' 110, *119*
Cycas revoluta 53, 57

D
Daignault, Cindy 186–96, *187–97*, 205, 206
Davallia solida var. *fejeensis* 16, 177, 196, 204
Demshak, Mark 108, *109–19*, 152–61
Dickenson, Melissa 122, *124–5*, 128
Dicksonia antarctica 14–15, 45, 54, 196
Dieffenbachia 16, 114, 165
Dionaea muscipula 218, *218*
Disocactus anguliger 136, *138*
Dracaena 128
   D. fragrans (Deremensis Group) 'Lemon Lime' 110, 173, *173*, 195
   D. fragrans (Deremensis Group) 'Warneckei' 127, 128
   D. marginata 122, *122–3*
   D. m. 'Tarzan' 188, *192*
   D. reflexa 59, 166, *169*
   D. trifasciata 16, 110, *128*, 181

E
Eames, Charles 165
Epiphyllum 40
   E. anguliger 36, 214, *214*
epiphytes 36, 212
Epipremnum aureum 16
   E. a. 'Neon' 177–8, *179*
   E. a. N'Joy 171, *171*
   E. pinnatum 'Cebu Blue' 128, 195, *195*
   E. p. Marble Planet 196, *197*
Euphorbia ingens 46, 57
   E. tirucalli 57
   E. trigona 134

F
Fassakhova, Alina *20*
Fay Ray Clay *26*, *30*
ferns 12, 15, 16, 36, 209
   asparagus 144, *144*
   austral gem *31*
   bird's nest 216, *216*
   Boston 144, 196, *197*
   crocodile 95, *148*, 171, 177, *180*, 185, 204
   kangaroo 165
   lemon button 196, *196–7*
   macho *145*, 148
   maidenhair *208*
   rabbit's foot 16, *36*, 177, 196, *196–7*, 204
   ribbon 171, *180*
   staghorn 30, 36, 45, 61, *204*, *204*, 206, 211, 214
Ficus 26
   F. benghalensis 'Audrey' 46, 195, *195*
   F. benjamina 154, *155*
   F. b. 'Danielle' *42*
   F. binnendijkii 'Alii' *43*, *44*, *148*, *149*
   F. elastica 22, 29, 42
   F. e. 'Burgundy' 14, 15, 124, *164*, 165
   F. lyrata 45, 46, *47*, 155, 166, *169*, 188
   F. retusa 42
   F. triangularis 50, 188, *193*
fig: fiddle-leaf 14, 46, 155, 166, *169*, 188
   weeping 154, *155*

G
Gem, Lolo *20*
Geogenanthus 206
Goeppertia insignis 219, *219*
   G. orbifolia 29, 181, 205, 213
Gonzalez-Torres, Felix 195
grouping 11
Guidera, Evan *42*

H
Harlan, Lane 130–2
Hatleberg, Curran 186–96, *187–97*, 205, 206
Hoya 36
   H. carnosa 16, *117*
Hyophorbe verschaffeltii 54
Hypnum curvifolium 36

222 INDEX

I
irrigation systems 32
Isennock, Megan and Rob 140–8, *141–51*

L
layering 11
lemon tree, Meyer *31*, 39
levels 11
light 12–16, *24*, 58, 143
lily, peace 128, *129*, 135
living walls 32–7

M
Makowski, John *45*, 205
Maranta leuconeura var. *erythroneura* 'Lemon Lime' 196
Marshall, Kerry James 42
materials 22–5
Mertz, Jose *16*, *21*
Mexico 130–2
Microsorum diversifolium 165
 M. musifolium 'Crocodyllus' *95*, *148*, *171*, *177*, *180*, *185*, 204
Millan, Pablo Antonio *160*
mint, Peruvian 116
money tree *160*, 171, *171*
monstera, mini 173
Monstera adansonii 122, 128, *133*, 135
 M. deliciosa 14, 143, 188, *192*, 195
 M. d. 'Albo Variegata' 68–71, *69–71*
moss 36, 211, *211*
Mount Vernon, Baltimore 174
Murillo, Elisa *158*

N
Neoregelia 'Bossa Nova' 171
 N. 'Hannibal Lecter' *92*, 93–5, *94–5*, 171
Nephrolepis biserrata 145, 148
 N. duffii 196
 N. exaltata 144
 N. e. 'Tiger Fern' 196

O
Odundo, Magdalene 86
Olea europaea 46, 165, *166*
olive tree 12, 46, 165, *166*
Opuntia 135, *136*
 O. ellisiana 57

orchids 12, 15, 36
outdoor glamour 52–61

P
Pachira aquatica *160*, 171
Pachypodium lamerei 29, 132
palm: bamboo 114, *116*, 155
 cat 122, *142*, 143
 fan 45, *45*, 53
 lady 166
 Madagascar 29, 132, *134*
 majestic 57, *142*, 148
 parlor 181, *182*, *203*, 215, *215*
 ponytail 12, 45, 57, 58, 132
 sago 53, 57
 spindle 54
pedestals 14–15, 48–51
Pemberton, Kevin 120–8, *121–9*
Peperomia 12, 26, 40, 209
 P. albovittata 209
 P. argyreia 16
 P. caperata 114, *119*
 P. c. 'Emerald Ripple' 195
 P. obtusifolia 59
 P. o. 'Variegata' *206*
 P. tetragona *119*, 165
Philodendron 115
 P. bernardopazii 54
 P. 'Birkin' 14, *27*, 39, 122, *182*, 185
 P. brandtianum 76–9, *77–9*
 P. giganteum 14
 P. 'Green Congo' 14, *117*
 P. 'Green Emerald' 143
 P. 'Imperial Green' *180*, 181
 P. 'Jungle Boogie' *26*
 P. 'McColley's Finale' 185, *185*
 P. melanochrysum 101–3, *101–3*
 P. 'Painted Lady' 188
 P. 'Rojo Congo' 15, *16*, *20*, *50*, 143
 P. rugosum 22
 P. selloum 110, *118*, *124*, 165, *176*, 177, 178–9, *179*, 181
 P. squamicaule 188, *192*
 P. tuxtlanum 'Tuxtla' 14
 P. xanadu 54, 155, *160*
Phlebodium aureum 'Blue Star' 114
Pierce, Matthew 130–2
pine, Norfolk Island 155, *156*, 185, *185*, 188
planters 26–31, 35, 210

Platycerium 30, 36
 P. bifurcatum 204
Pollock, Jackson 90
Polyscias 'Fabian' 177, *179*
Portulacaria afra 196
pothos 195, *195*
 marble queen 16
 moonlight 16
 neon 177–8, *179*
 N'Joy 171, *171*
 satin 16
prayer plant 110
prickly pear 135, *136*
propagation 35
Pteris cretica 171, *180*

R
Raba, Carlos 130–2
Radermachera sinica 173, *173*, 188
Raphidophora tetrasperma 134–5
rattlesnake plant 213, 219, *219*
Ravenea rivularis 57, *142*, 148
Ray, Fay *42*
Revival Baltimore 174–85, *175–85*
Rhaphidophora tetrasperma *172*, 173
Rhapis excelsa 166
rubber tree 22, 29, 39, 42, 124
 burgundy 14, 15, *164*, 165, 166

S
Sansevieria sayuri *206*
 S. trifasciata 'Futura Robusta' 171
 S. t. var. *laurentii* 128
Sargent, John Singer 106
Schefflera 188
Scindapsus pictus 'Argyraeus' 16
 S. treubii 'Moonlight' 16
Shakespeare, William 174, 177
Sherald, Amy 120–8, *121–9*
snake plant 16, 50, 110, 128, *128–9*, 171, 181
Song of India 59, 166, *169*
Spathiphyllum 128
 S. wallisii 135
spider plant *203*, 217, *217*
statement plants 42–7
Stein, Irena 53, 108–19, *109–19*, 152–61

Strelitzia 46
 S. reginae 15, 181
string of hearts 221, *221*
Stromanthe sanguinea 'Triostar' *111*, 220, *220*
succulents 12, 40, 53, 54, *54–5*, 58, *61*
Swiss cheese plant 188, *192*

T
terrariums *31*, 196, *196*, *203*, 208–9, *208–9*
textures 22
Tillandsia 36, 196, 204, 212, *212*
 T. cyanea 36
 T. streptophylla 212
tree ferns 45
 Australian 14–15, *40*, 46, 54, 196, *196–7*
Triostar stromanthe *111*, 220, *220*

U
umbrella plant 188

V
Venezuela 110, 152–61
Venus flytrap 218, *218*
vine plants 16, *79*, *102*, *126*, *133*, *164*, 165, 221, *221*
Voss, Barbara *61*

W
Wearstler, Kelly 86
Weininger, Bridget *45*, 205
wood 25
Wool, Christopher 195

Y
yucca 136, *137*, *139*, *142*, 143

Z
Zamioculcas zamiifolia 16, 165, 173, *204*
Zhang, Pamela *190*
ZZ plant 16, 165, 173, *204*

THANKS AND LOVE

I am beyond grateful for yet another opportunity to share my passion for indoor greenery with those of you who feel the same love and enthusiasm. As I have with every book I've created, let me start by thanking my incredibly warm and loving wife, Fiona, because without her I'd surely be lost in the world. Fiona, your love for me is a fierce beam of light. I can't express in words how you help me be as productive as I am, as loving as I am, and, now, the father that I am. Thank you. To all my family and friends that have been so supportive through everything, thank you.

Irena and Mark, thank you for giving me the time and space to work a little magic in your home and also at Alma Cocina. The beauty you've created in these spaces is a reflection of who you both are as people. Amy and Kevin, thank you for trusting me to bring a lushness to your home that spoke to your aesthetics perfectly. Megan and Rob, thank you for letting me play in your pool while plant styling your outdoor space. Shawn and Anne, thank you for opening your home to me and providing the perfect canvas to plant style. And Cindy and Curran, thank you for being patient as I figured out what would work best in your beautiful home. I hope you love how it all came together as much as I do. To the team at Revival Baltimore, thank you for the opportunity to bring your lobby to life—I'm looking forward to our next project together. Lane, Carlos, and Matthew, thank you for being so gracious and opening the doors of Clavel so I could add an extra touch of Mexico. And Sienna, Tarana, Bridget, John, Evan, Fay, Jamie, Drury, and Stephanie—thank you. Your homes were already so special and I feel honored to have be a small part of what has made them so wonderful.

To have been fortunate enough to make one book, let alone four, is just incredible. I couldn't have plant styled the spaces in this book without the help of Logan Doll and the *green neighbor* team: Nijol, Autumn, Sarah, and Emma. Thank you. To the amazing team at CICO Books, thank you for being patient with me on this one. It took longer than we thought, but it was so worth it. Thank you for the hard work all of you put in to make our fourth book together a success. Let's keep it going.

Lastly, to all of you in the green loving community who have embarked on this journey in greenery with me, thank you. Your support and encouragement has motivated me throughout the process of making my books. I hope you've found inspiration within the pages of this book to style your home, or the homes of others, in a way that is impactful, creative and, of course, wild.

CREDITS

Hilton Carter
@hiltoncarter
thingsbyhc.com

STYLED SPACES

Mixed Greens
@almacocinalatina
almacocinalatina.com

Artist's Statement
@asherald
@mr_pemberton

A Gathered Space
@revivalbaltimore
revivalbaltimore.com

Wood Grains and Concrete Plains
@bar_clavel
barclavel.com

Poetic Planting
@ai_rei_rei
almacocinalatina.com

Neighbors
@shawn_chopra
@goodneighborshop
goodneighborshop.com

Untitled (The Painter and the Photographer)
@cynthia_daignault
@_suttree_
cynthiadaignault.com
curranhatleberg.com

Room with a View
@meganisennock
with styling help from
Adel Ainslie @life_of_reily

ADDITIONAL SPACES

Tarana J. Burke
@taranajaneen
metoomvmt.org

Evan Guidera and Fay Ray
@illwigpiece
@fayraystudio
fay-ray.com

Bridget Weininger and John Makowski
@bridget_weininger
@john_mako_____

Stephanie Bradshaw
@sbcreative_
stephanie-bradshaw.com

Barbara Voss
@hedgerow.shop
hedgerowshop.com

Jamie Campbell and Drury Bynum
@jamiecampbellbynum
@drurybynum

PLANTERS

Fay Ray Clay
@fayrayclay
fayrayclay.com

Cay Ceramics
@cay_ceramics
cayceramics.com

Pamela Zhang
@pamelazhang
pamelazhang.store

Personal Best Ceramics
@personalbestceramics
personalbestceramics.com

green neighbor
@greenneighborshop
greenneighborshop.com

Hilton Carter for Target
@hiltoncarter
@target

PEDESTALS

Area Fabrication
@areafabrication
areafabrication.com

Hilton Carter for Target
@hiltoncarter
@target

Majer Metal Works
@majermetalworks
majermetalworks.com